The Stone Canoe

and other stories

The Stone Canoe

and other stories

written and illustrated
by

John L. Peyton

The McDonald & Woodward Publishing Company
Blacksburg, Virginia
1989

The McDonald & Woodward Publishing Company
P. O. Box 10308, Blacksburg, Virginia 24062–0308

The Stone Canoe and other stories

© 1989 by The McDonald & Woodward Publishing Company

All rights reserved. First printing, 1989
Composition by Marathon Typesetting, Roanoke, Virginia
Printed in the United States of America
by BookCrafters, Chelsea, Michigan, USA

96 95 94 93 92 91 90   10 9 8 7 6 5 4 3 2 1

Map on back cover:

This map is based on information taken from NTS Map Sheet 52–I

© 1987. Her Majesty the Queen in Right of Canada with permission of Energy, Mines and Resources Canada.

Library of Congress Cataloging–in–Publication Data

Peyton, John L., 1907–
      The stone canoe and other stories / written and illustrated by John L. Peyton.
          p.   cm.
      ISBN 0–939923–06–8 : $24.95. — ISBN 0–939923–07–6 (pbk.). : $14.95
      1. Ojibwa Indians—Legends. 2. Indians of North America—Great Lakes Region
—Legends. I. Title.
E99.C6P49   1989
398.2'08997—dc19   89-2294
                                                                       CIP

"The Enemy" is excerpted from the unpublished manuscript "Faces in the Firelight."

Contents

Preface

I remember the People of the Rapids, the northern-most Anishinabeg (Ojibway). They were tough and self-reliant, but they laughed a lot. Sometimes they kidded each other roughly, especially when they were cold or hungry, which was quite often.

Their winters were too long and their hills too stony for primitive agriculture. They depended for their lives on the shifting patterns of fish and game that were sometimes inexplicably plentiful and again faded into nothing.

When the deer and the rabbits disappeared, the wolves and the lynxes starved. And then, if the ice froze too deep for netting, men, women and children knew the horror of famine.

That suffering showed in the legends. Punishment came down on those who failed to respect the animals they hunted, or who killed more meat than they could eat or save. Virtue was rewarded with a shower of fish, rather than of gold, as in European fairy tales. In a bad winter, skull-faced Windigo, the specter of cannibalism, prowled through the spruce at the edge of the clearing. But always, there were the clowns and the laughter.

Old men and old women made certain that these stories did not die, but were continued on through the young to those not yet born. In this way they preserved remembrance and pride in achievements of the ancestors, the ancient wisdom and bitter humor of the subarctic forest, and a code of behavior that had to be followed, without the pressure of reward or punishment, if the people were to survive.

During some seasons two or more families would live together in one lodge. Almost everybody witnessed, in early childhood, sex, birth, occasional violence between men, undernourishment, sickness and death. These events, familiar, but still awesome and mysterious, were important in their folktales.

When I asked to hear more of the old legends I was referred to Grandma Wadikwan. There seemed to be no limit to her supply.

The old lady told her stories in lively, informal words, keeping their basic structures unchanged while she added embellishments of her own. She acted out some parts and accompanied others with gestures, her hands swaying in the smoky firelight. She spoke in a low, masculine voice for a man and higher for a woman. As she talked, she would sometimes fashion little figures of grass, sticks, or bark and move them to illustrate the action.

She spoke freely of bodily parts, wastes, and functions. Nobody was embarrassed or offended at the mention of such cosmic essentials.

She drew only vague lines between men and animals, natural and supernatural. A character might wander back and forth across those lines leaving the listeners uncertain as to whether this was human or something else.

She didn't explain the meanings, some simple, some profound, that were hidden in the stories. These were secret things that each person had to search out for himself.

But she had a fine feeling for the effective pause. At the proper moment she would put the pipe back in her mouth and sit with hands folded, watching the faces of her audience. When she judged that they understood and appreciated her meaning, she would continue.

In retelling these tales I have used drawings in place of the grandmother's gestures, lay figures, and pantomime. I can't give you the timed delays nor the hand- and smoke-work. In other respects I will try to pass the stories along in the same way that she did, but in present-day language and idiom.

The forest people have it easier now. They are multiplying and fattening under the protection of the welfare state. No more sunken-eyed children with bloated bellies.

But something of the old life, something important, is missing. It has disappeared, like a decorated basket that is laid on blazing logs to writhe, blacken, and be gone, leaving just the pungent smoke of birch-bark and porcupine-quill embroidery.

I hope that these stories will give some understanding of the woods Indians that I knew—men and women with the wit and courage to survive whenever survival was possible, and, when it was not, to laugh a little, and then to die quietly, without self-pity, like the wolves and the deer.

J. L. P.

The Stone Canoe

A shower of pebbles rolled and bounced down the cliff. Starsound ducked her head and raised a sheltering arm as they splashed around the canoe, and rattled against its cedar frame.

"Careful up there! You might loosen a big one."

Here-she-comes looked down and smiled.

"If I did, I'd come to you with it. So I'll be careful. And don't worry about a little dirt on your head, sister-friend. It will make your hair grow."

She stopped speaking and moved sideways along the face of the cliff—across the stone palisade that carries the forest on its shoulders and stands, waist-deep in the big water, 'Tshgumi.

The rock was cold, but she pressed against it, spread out flat as a creeping chipmunk. She had left her moccasins in the canoe. Her toes, long and supple as thumbs, were searching their way, feeling out and gripping an almost invisible ledge. Her fingers were clinging to each crack in the wall, each runt of a tree or spindly bush that drew life from the face of the rock.

Something else grew here—a rare and modest little plant whose healing roots were needed by the medicine woman. They must be gathered under just these conditions, as a strong wind died at evening, while the cliff still dripped from the waves, and foam streaked the dark water below.

When she reached a clump of the healing flowers, Here-she-comes spoke to them softly, explaining that they would be used to ease the misery of poor old Uncle Thunder. Then she drew a knife from a sheath strapped to her leg, cautiously dug

1

into the chink, loosened the sacred things and dropped them into a bag at her belt.

When she had the needed quantity she crept farther along to where the ledge widened a little above a buttress, a pillar of stone that stood at a bend in the cliff. Here, she had to let go her handholds to tie the bag shut. So she pressed even tighter against the rock, feeling its chill and the crusty texture of the lichens through her thin dress.

Starsound watched anxiously, shifting her grip on the rock, holding the canoe steady while it rose and fell on easing swells. She did not fear these drowsy rollers, the aftermath of the storm. But this was not a place to stay any longer than you had to.

There were no escape-openings in the sheer wall of granite. Only the caves.

The waves had long ago reached down to the bottom of the lake for boulders, and used them to batter and grind out these caverns, and even tunnels that ran nobody knew how far back into the stone and under the forest.

Waves with power like that would crush any canoe that they could trap here. And nobody knew when hostile wind-and water-spirits might fling another storm across the great lake.

"You have what is needed, sister-friend. Come down now and let us get get back to the fishing camp."

Here-she-comes made the gesture for silence. She had her hands free again to grip the cliff and had edged still farther around the bend.

She was staring at something out there beyond. Then, she turned quickly and worked her way back to the crevice where she had climbed. As she came sliding and checking down its chute she spoke in low, excited tones.

"I have seen the little people! They looked up at me. They waved to me with their arms. They wanted us to come. Then they paddled into a cave."

She eased into the stern, took up her paddle, and pushed out from the rock. With strong, short strokes she got the canoe quickly under way. Starsound sat rigid in the bow.

"Come on, help me. We must follow them."

"Humans should stay away from the Maymaygwashiwog. They are covered with hair and have no noses. They move over the water in stone canoes. They laugh at us from inside the solid cliffs. They steal fish from our nets. Sometimes they throw rocks. They can raise up a storm, any time they want to,

2

by singing a magic song. They bring misfortune on anyone who hurts or hinders them. And what will Moosefoot say if he knows that you have followed them?"

"We're not going to hurt or hinder any of them. And as for Moosefoot, he's had plenty of time to say anything he wanted to say to me. And he hasn't said it. So get busy. Now we must work together."

Reluctantly Starsound picked up her paddle. They came around the pile of granite fragments that ran out from the foot of the buttress.

Beyond stretched the precipice, narrowing away, fading into distant mists, broken only by masses of stone that the lake had torn away from it and then stacked up against it. And by the dark mysteries of caves.

Starsound laid her paddle across the gunwales. "Nobody comes this far along the palisades. The women don't set nets here. This is not a place for people."

Paddling strongly, Here-she-comes drove the canoe ahead. She swept it past an outcropping where an ancient cedar crouched, reaching down at them with long and twisted arms. They bent low, but Starsound felt the sharp points tug at her hair and scrape along her shoulder. Then Here-she-comes ruddered hard and they swung into darkness.

Starsound could hear the belch and grumble of waves reverberating from far back in the cave like the snorts of some ancient monster. Slabs of rock, bigger than any wigwam, hung from the ceiling. Looking down, she could see other slabs in the clear water below.

"Sister," she whispered. "Great rocks have fallen from above us. Others may drop at any moment."

"Not in this quiet evening," said Here-she-comes. "It would take stronger waves than these to bring them down." Then she leaned forward and called, "We are here, Maymaygwashiwog."

They sat in silence. Then a paddle scraped against stone behind them. They turned and saw a canoe silhouetted dark against the daylight. It seemed to be coming out of the rock.

It moved toward them quickly, long and low in the water, driven by the strokes of many little paddlers. As they approached the girls they began to jabber excitedly. One of them stood up, waving his arms and jumping about so that the canoe tilted dangerously. Hair grew down over his face like an otter's, almost covering his lips. They could just make out his words.

"Welcome, welcome. Welcome to the rock world. At last, humans have come to us. You will be our sisters and our mothers and our aunties. And tell us what to do and we will do it. And show us how to shed the fur off our faces and grow tall like you Indians, and with big, beautiful noses."

"We could not change your size or your faces," said Here-she-comes. "But you look pretty good to me the way you are."

A wave of smiles swept along the line of hairy little boatmen, lifting the otter whiskers. Paddles stirred, moving closer.

Starsound could smell them now, smoky and sweaty as men, but with a fishy flavor. And she could see that the canoe was made of stone.

Starsound gripped her paddle. "Sister," she moaned, "let us leave this place."

"Oh, do not go away," cried the the spokesman. "Stay with us and we will feed you so many fine trout that you will grow fat and glossy. You will never be hungry again."

A squeaky new voice shouted, "If you try to leave us we'll throw rocks and sink you."

Here-she-comes's blade churned white water in the darkness. The little people dug with their paddles, striving to get their heavy craft into swift motion. The spokesman struggled to keep his balance, then fell heavily among those behind him, rocking the boat and breaking the quickening rhythm of the stroke. The bark canoe shot past them.

No rocks were thrown—only a dismal wail.

At the mouth of the cave Here-she-comes checked speed, then swung the canoe sideways.

The speaker was on his feet again, holding out his arms.

"Stay with us and you will always be young and beautiful."

"How about that, Starsound?"

"No, no, no! I want to go back to my own people."

"You go then. I'll stay."

Here-she-comes untied the bag of roots from her belt and tossed it toward the bow. She put on her moccasins, took up her paddle, and brought the canoe back alongside the other. A dozen crooked hands clawed it, holding the two boats locked together. Here-she-comes stood up, put a hand on a hairy little shoulder, and stepped across the gunwales.

"Let go," she ordered, and the bark canoe floated clear.

Starsound had swiveled around and was on her knees, keeping the paddle ready while she shifted her weight to balance the empty length of the canoe. Now she surged the blade into the water in a mighty stroke. The strain was too sharp for cedar. The shaft cracked like a broken bone.

She leaned forward and grabbed the paddle that Here-she-comes had laid down. Her strokes were shorter now, a little more cautious, but speeding and strengthening as the canoe picked up speed. She shot it out of the cave without once looking back. Drove it, punishing herself unmercifully, past the long lines of the palisades. She did not relent until the smell of smoke came drifting out on the warm land breeze from the cooking fires at camp. Then she slumped forward, breathing hard, pulling herself together, wondering whether it had really happened.

5

Everyone marvelled at her story but nobody doubted it. She was a heroine—she had seen the Maymaygwashiwog. But, oh, women, wail for poor Here-she-comes.

Moosefoot did not wail, but he mourned through several silent days for his lost love. Then he brought gifts to Starsound's parents. When these were accepted he spoke up at last and asked her to be his wife.

They had a boy and three girls, a large family for those times. But he was a good hunter and she was thrifty. They raised every one of the children, somehow shooting or snaring or digging out enough food for all, even in the worst winters.

The years passed and there were many grandchildren.

And more years. Moosefoot died, satisfied with life and content to leave it. The children's hair grew gray. They and their children died or moved away, all except one granddaughter. Starsound lived on in this woman's lodge, well cared for by her and her husband.

Then came the long, dry summer. The berries were small and the stalks of wild rice had only thin, hard kernels that rattled in the wind.

When the snow fell it showed no hoof-prints. The rabbit snares stood alert, eager, and empty. It was a time of great cold, but also of savage winds. On still nights the lake would freeze far out, but in the morning he would roar in anger and tear the covering away, leaving dark water that moaned and foamed almost to the shore.

All through the first part of that winter the father carried his canoe across the frozen strip, took his chances with the waves and the ice, and brought back enough herring so that the family could eat fairly well. Then, when the days began to lengthen, the fish disappeared as mysteriously as the deer. He lifted the nets and found nothing. So he went no more to the water.

In the darkness before each dawn he took his musket and walked into the forest. On most evenings he returned without meat, but sometimes he brought a weasel, a jaybird, or a skinny porcupine. He laughed as he handed these poor creatures to his wife, but she divided them carefully, making sure that her grandmother, as well as each of the children, got a little something almost every night.

Not enough, though. Starsound could see that the heads were becoming skulls. One morning she slipped out of the lodge as soon as the father left it, and called him back.

"I will leave you now," she told him. "I can't do any real work and I don't want to eat more of the children's food."

"That is kind of you, grandmother," he said. "Maybe we can keep them alive until the ducks come back and the sweet sap runs in the maples. If that happens, they will be grateful to you, and you will live in them and in their children."

He walked on up the trail into the hills. She went down to where 'Tschgumi had hurled up great blocks of ice. They lay, or stood upended, like a little mountain range with the dark blue water showing through between the peaks.

She walked along down the snow-covered surface between this barrier and the shore. She wanted to go a long way, to get to some far-off place where the children would not be likely to find her before the lake took her back with its ice.

But her knees became unwilling to carry her farther. They wanted to fold, and they didn't care much if that would dump her into the snow.

She told them that she weighed almost nothing now, and that surely they could hold up that skinny body a little longer. "All right," they answered, "but only a few more steps."

She turned toward the lake and climbed the frozen ridges. When she came out on a ledge already undercut by the water she took off her snowshoes, placed them side by side, and sank down on them.

The sun was bright but a wind from the lake bit through her clothing. She thought that she would not have to wait long.

She dozed, dreaming of things that had happened long ago. It seemed natural that Here-she-comes should be speaking to her again.

"Wake up, Starsound. I have brought you a gift."

She was standing there, young and beautiful as she had been in the dream. She was holding out a fat black trout. Hairy faces peered out from around her skirts. Other Maymay-gwashiwog stood on the edge of the ice, their paddles holding the canoe.

The old woman siezed the fish, her eyes gleaming. She raised it, holding it before her open mouth. The remnants of her worn and broken teeth were ready to tear the sweet flesh. But she stopped as though she were already frozen. Then she lowered the trout and tried to get up on the snowshoes.

"You need not carry it back," said the girl. "They have meat now at your granddaughter's lodge. Her man has killed a deer. So eat."

7

Starsound bit down, gumming and crunching the fish, feeling life surge back into her body. Soon Here-she-comes laid a hand on her arm.

"Wait a little, sister-friend. Don't sicken your empty stomach with too much too soon."

Starsound stopped eating and rested for a few moments. She gazed at Here-she-comes.

"The Maymaygwashiwog kept their promises. You have put on weight since I saw you last, and you are as beautiful as you were then, but you are no older." She took another bite.

Here-she-comes smiled. "I will pass part of that blessing on to you. I can't make you young, but I can make you fat. When you go back, tell them to set out the nets. The fish have returned."

The women sat together on the snowshoes. Starsound finished the trout. At a signal from Here-she-comes, one of the little men brought her another.

Starsound untied her belt thong, slipped it through the gills and tied it back around her waist. Here-she-comes helped her to her feet and bound on her snowshoes.

"I will take this one to the lodge," said Starsound. "I believe you, but just in case he happened to miss that deer. Will I see you again?"

"No, sister, we will go back now into the rock. We laugh there and are happy."

The paddlers took their places. Here-she-comes stepped neatly down among them. Starsound watched the stone canoe move fast over the water and disappear behind a mass of ice.

She walked slowly back toward camp, resting often. Shadows lengthened out from the coastal hills, moved across the snow toward the lake, and climbed the sides of the frozen mountains.

Far ahead on the pale blue surface, a dark figure was hurrying, following her tracks. After a while she could see that it was her granddaughter's husband. He came up, smiling.

"I am happy to find you still alive, grandmother. Now you will not need to die for a while."

His blood-stained hand held out a piece of venison. She took his knife, cut off a little of the fattest part and ate it.

When they came to the steep place where the trail left the shore he held out his hand to her again and helped her up over the rocks as though she were a little girl.

Give-Away Woman

Snow was falling into the Lake of the Islands, a white rim of ice was forming around the rocks of its shore, and the fire felt good. The women held out their hands to it, hands that were chilled from the water and slimy-scaly from fish. But they did not rest long.

Heron and her oldest daughter carried up the canoe and prepared the catch, splitting each whitefish into two neat sections. The two younger sisters hung these pieces on the racks over the fire. Old lady Nokomis brought in some wood and poked at the embers from time to time. She was trying to be helpful, but she was getting in the way more than she was helping. Her little grandson, Nanabush, not long out of his cradle board, was chewing on a piece of fish that one of the girls had given him.

"Give me some of those whitefish," said Nokomis.

Heron picked up a small jackfish-pickerel and handed it to her.

"I will need more than this," said Nokomis. "Nanabush is little but already he eats a lot. And winter is coming on."

"I'm sorry," said Heron. "I have only enough for my own family, so I will not give you any more. Go and catch some for yourself."

"I am too old and too cold to tend the nets."

"Then you had better snare some rabbits."

"But Mother," said the oldest daughter, "there is no fat on rabbits. We can catch more fish tomorrow."

"How do you know what we will catch tomorrow? The whitefish come in herds like the caribou deer and they can go like the deer, all together and far away, to nobody knows where. Tomorrow our nets may hang empty in the water. Besides, your father and your brother have already gone on to the winter hunting camp, and we must pack the canoe and follow them before the rivers freeze. We have only a few more days for fishing. We will need all that we catch."

The girl sharpened her knife, then sliced another fish and tossed it to her sisters.

"But Mother," she said, "it is not the custom to leave old people and the very young without food for the winter."

"My custom," said Heron, "is to eat regularly and to make sure that you and the rest of my family eat too."

Nanabush spoke then in a piping little voice, but clearly. "You'd better give Noko more fish, or you'll be sorry."

"So," said Heron, "the baby threatens me. It was bad enough to get backtalk from my daughter. Now it comes from someone who still has to be packed in moss for the night. That is going to be a very sassy little boy, Nokomis. You had better take him back to your own lodge. I will give no more fish."

Nokomis took the pickerel in one hand and Nanabush with the other, and walked away.

Heron looked up at the night sky. One by one, the stars were winking out. A little wind riffled the water of the lake and sighed in the spruces overhead.

"A storm is coming," she said. "Cut poles to brace the lodge and the drying racks while I cover the fish."

It turned out to be a worse storm than she had ever seen. It blew down the racks in spite of the bracing and scattered the fish in the bush. Heron and her girls couldn't find them in the dark. The small animals did, though, and there were none left at daylight.

Heron told the oldest daughter to get some dried meat to cook for breakfast. When the girl climbed up to the cache they heard her give a little cry of sorrow. "A wolverine has broken in," she called. "He has eaten almost everything and has dirtied what he couldn't eat."

The water was so rough that they were unable to tend the nets that day or the next. Then a great cold came and the lake froze, even though the wind was still blowing.

"See," said Heron. "Mother knows best. It's well that I didn't give away any more fish. I only wish I had that pickerel back.

"Now we must get on to the hunting camp. The river will still be open. I will carry the canoe to it. You girls pack up and follow me."

But the wind tore the canoe from her shoulders. It flew through the air like a crazy grouse and broke its back against a stump.

Heron and her daughters set snares along the rabbit trails. For the next three weeks they lived on rabbits. They got tired of rabbit.

One day they heard the creak of snowshoes. The hunters had returned pulling an empty toboggan.

"We came back to get the fish and to find out why you hadn't followed us," said Heron's husband, Thunder-in-the-Night. "There were plenty of deer until the storm. After that we didn't see any. Maybe somebody has broken an important regulation."

"Then you must have done something wrong at camp," said Heron. "Because I gave the old lady a nice pickerel."

"Was that all you gave her?" Thunder-in-the-Night picked up some rabbits that the girls had brought in that morning and hurried to the wigwam of Nokomis.

"My wife sends you these, grandmother," he said. "She will bring you more tomorrow, and meat of the first deer if I shoot any. I will see that you and the baby don't lack for venison all winter, if I have any. But maybe we will all starve. We can't live very long in cold weather like this on just rabbits."

Nanabush sat up in his hammock and spoke. "Go back to Heron's wigwam and set out all the bark boxes and the willow baskets."

"But this wind will blow them away," said Thunder-in-the-Night. Then he stopped and listened. The roar of the storm had ended.

"And any other containers you can find," said Nanabush. "Even turn the broken canoe right side up. Stay in the lodge until morning. Your give-away woman will want the minks and the skunks to get their share."

That night they heard things thumping outside and in the morning all the containers they had set out were full of split and dried whitefish. The small animals, of course, had stuffed themselves, but this time there was so much that all they took made hardly any difference.

Thunder-in-the-Night and his family started for their winter quarters in the hills, but had gone only a little way when a fat caribou came out of the woods and stood looking at them. Thunder shot it. Heron skinned it, split it, and carried a half back to Nokomis' wigwam.

Nobody in either camp was hungry that winter.

The Flame Thief

A long time ago, before the Indians had fire, they used to get pretty cold at night. Nanabush showed them how to wrap themselves in animal fur and how to sew the pelts together into coats and fur blankets. They were happy to have these, at first.

But one winter night, as they huddled under the skin coverings, a man groaned a little and then spoke in a shivery voice.

"These hairy old hides are better than nothing, but they itch. And I'm still cold."

A woman answered out of the darkness.

"You would think that anybody who is supposed to have so much power could keep his people warm. That shouldn't be too much to ask."

Nanabush went back to his grandmother's lodge, laid down on the bough bedding and pulled a beaver robe over his head. The ice kept forming on the fur around his nose, and his feet were almost freezing. He whispered, "Grandma, how long until spring?"

There was no answer, and he spoke louder.

"You can't be sleeping, Nokomis, because it's too cold. So answer me. How many days until the crows come back?"

"I already told you. Yesterday I showed you my time stick. I've cut the notches only a little way along it. Asking so often just makes the winter pass more slowly."

After a while she spoke again.

"When I was a girl up there in the lodge of my father, the moon, we had fire. That gave light and kept everybody warm."

"What did you feed it?"

"Birch bark and dry cedar while it was young. It grew faster than any other living thing. Soon we gave it pieces of stumps and trees. It loved pine pitch best of all. Whenever I fed it some of that it jumped for joy and sent up a lot of black smoke. We had a hole in the roof to let that go out of the lodge."

"Did the fire creature ever get mean?"

"It didn't like to be touched. If we touched it, it would bite.

"It bit me once and left a spot on my arm that hurt. My mother mixed bear's grease and balsam balm and put it on the sore place. After a while it was well again."

There was another time of silence. Then Nanabush pushed aside his skin covering and sat up.

"Noko, I'm going to get some of that thing. That fire thing that keeps people warm. Bring in the bark and the wood."

"Nanabush, don't you even dare to think of it. The giant, Misabe, has the fire now. He would kill you."

"Cut a hole in the roof. And have ready some of the grease that makes the sore place well again. Have a lot of it."

He went outside, broke open a pine stump and scraped off some pitch. Then he changed himself into a wabooz, a long-legged hare, all white except for black eartips. He rubbed the pitch into his tail and went hopping off over the drifts. He jumped higher and higher until he was able to hook his front paws over the edge of the sky.

He hung there for a while, spying out the country. Ahead was a broad expanse of snow. Beyond that he could see a long, uneven mass that would have to be timbered hills.

After a while he caught sight of a little light in the jagged line of darkness. It glowed and disappeared. He watched that place closely, and the light came again. He climbed up on the sky and hopped toward it.

It was a lodge like his grandmother's, but much bigger. Pines had been laid against it, their branches locked together, to hold the bark covering in place. Every so often a flickering light shone from a smoke-hole at the top. The door was covered by a robe of moose hides. He slipped under it and into the glare and warmth of fire.

The first thing he saw was an infant almost as big as Nokomis. It was watching him from a cradle-board hung on a tree trunk that had been bent and twisted to serve as one of the lodge-poles. An enormous woman was stretching a bearskin over a plank frame as easily as though it were a mink pelt on a board. Nanabush hopped toward her and shivered.

"Why, you poor little wabooz," she said. "You look cold. Warm yourself, but don't get too close to the fire. My husband is always afraid that somebody will steal it."

Nanabush turned his back toward the blaze. The heat felt good. He edged a little nearer, watching the woman. She came over to stir a simmering kettle, looked down at him and spoke sharply.

"That will be close enough."

Just then the door covering swung up. A giant poked his head inside. He stopped there on hands and knees, pushed long, matted, hair away from his face, and looked around the lodge. His nose wrinkled and his big, wet nostrils spread wide, twitching. Then he crawled in, stood up, and roared.

"Haw! Ho! Hi! Hun! I smell the blood of an Indian!"

"There are no Indians here, Misabe. There are only the baby and I and this cold little wabooz that wants to get warm."

"I'll fix that. I'll put him into the stew-kettle. That'll warm you, Wabooz-Indian."

He stepped quickly toward the hare, stooping, feet wide apart, big fingers curling to grab.

Nanabush jumped back. He felt the heat close behind his heels. He reached out his tail, stretching it far.

There was a puff and a burst of flame. He took off, scorching Misabe's legs, blasting the moose skin straight out from the lodge poles and leaving a trail like a fiery comet.

His wide wabooz feet thumped hard against the crust. He sailed over the drifts, speeded by hurt of the burning and by loud footsteps pounding behind. As they neared the edge the giant swung his war club. Its head, a great pointed boulder, crashed down. It would have caught and crushed any ordinary hare, but this one was the son of the westwind and the great-grandson of the moon. He dodged with supernatural agility. The club missed, struck the sky and broke off a piece of it.

Nanabush was over the edge, falling, falling. Misabe threw the club. It hurtled, spinning, past the laid-back cars. The giant's roars grew fainter until they were only thunder in the winter sky.

Nokomis had the kindling ready and was holding the door covering open. The other Indians had come out of the wigwams to watch. Their faces gleamed in the firelight as Nanabush flared by.

He squatted over the curl of birch bark just long enough to make sure that it had caught the flame.

"Put on the cedar, Noko," he shouted, and bounded out of the lodge. He shot across the campground to a flying sit in deep snow. The fire hissed like seven angry snakes and went out.

Nanabush changed himself into a man again and limped back into the lodge.

He lay on his face while Nokomis bathed the burns with cold water and put wet compresses on them. Later she rubbed in a mixture of bear's grease and balsam balm.

All this time people were coming in with rolls of birch bark and carrying out pieces of fire. No matter how much they took away, there was always plenty of it left. Soon each lodge was sending a shaft of light up from its smokehole into the cold darkness.

Everybody agreed that this hot, bright, beautiful stuff would keep the people alive and warm in even the coldest winter. And that Nanabush looked silly, sprawled out in the bedding with the old lady rubbing grease on his bottom.

That was how we stole fire from heaven.

Black Spruce

1

A long time ago there was a wicked magician who had two beautiful and virtuous daughters. They lived in the forest north of 'Tschgumi. Their wigwam was sheltered from the lake storms by a granite ridge timbered with stunted and wind-torn black spruce. It is said that the witch doctor's sorcery was as dark and twisted as those tattered old trees.

The girls were beautiful, all right, no one could dispute that, but they were getting a little elderly to be still living in the parental lodge.

Whenever a young man came bringing gifts for either of them, their father, Middlehawk, walked up to the summit of the ridge, laid out his conjure kit, and sat there under the crooked trees, beating on a drum, chanting destructive songs, and wrapping a net of incantation around the victim.

One suitor broke through the ice and almost drowned. Another went hungry for a long time because none of the animals would allow him to catch them. A third felt a crick come into his back. The last they saw of him, he was hobbling away, leaning on a stick like an arthritic old man.

Then there was that unlucky hunter who was knocked down and run over by a wounded moose. The cow, terrified and seeking only to escape, ran blindly through the willow thicket where he was standing and sent him flying into the swamp. His arm struck a stump and he heard the bone snap. Middlehawk set it and wrapped it in a birch bark cast, but it healed at an odd angle.

Rednecklace, the first daughter, was thinking about these happenings as she scraped a stretched beaver skin. She wasn't

getting much meat off, but she was reaching some conclusions about her father. At length indignation overcame her usual modesty, and she spoke to him boldly.

"We might have thought that the moose trick was just an accident, if it hadn't been for all those other accidents. But I happen to know that you can do a better job of bone-setting than that. It would have been enough to just break the arm. That would have sent him on his way. You didn't have to set it crooked too."

She jabbed a few vicious strokes at the pelt, then turned back to the silent sorcerer.

"You always make things happen to any man who comes to visit Sandcherry or me. They go away and they don't come back. And word gets around. How are we ever going to find husbands if you keep on treating our friends like that?"

Middlehawk looked at her sadly, but with deep affection.

"You remind me of your mother when you get angry."

He paused a moment, a faraway melancholy in his eyes. Then he went on.

"None of those guys was half good enough for either of you. They weren't our kind of people. Besides, if you marry, who will butcher and cook my venison? Who will bring wood for my fire? Who will dress my hair? Who, I ask you, will tend my net and make my moccasins?"

"Sandy is good at every one of those things. So please, father, give me a break. Cast no spells on the next man who comes here looking for a wife. Then I, the older daughter, will go away with him."

At that there was a wail from Sandcherry. "I could never handle all those chores alone."

"You are quite right, my dear," said Middlehawk. "There is much work to be done and I'm afraid that your sister is being just a little selfish. Up here in the northern woods, every lodge needs two good women.

"But my years are passing swiftly. Soon I will walk the trail of the spirits. Then you will forget your old father and each of you will go her own way."

He stopped speaking and bowed his head, overcome by emotion.

Rednecklace snorted like a startled doe.

"For a long time I hoped for that piece of good fortune. But I've given up even thinking about it now. You just get meaner and healthier every year. You will still be doing your witch work when I'm a shriveled old woman."

"Well I, for one, don't intend to stay in this lodge forever," said Sandcherry. "I'm going to marry somebody and get out of here."

They went on grumbling and threatening like that day after day. Rednecklace kept cutting at the poor old father with the sharp edge of her tongue. Sandcherry sulked without mercy and every so often burst out in sassy backtalk.

This nagging and pouting got more and more unpleasant, especially during the moon of the little ghosts. The snow is getting deep then, and the nights are the longest of the year. People are cutting down on their eating to make the food last through until spring. They have to spend a lot of time in the lodge together and each person is supposed to be extra kind to everybody else.

One morning, just as a little light was beginning to show in the smoke opening overhead, Rednecklace reached out and pressed Sandcherry's cheek.

"Daylight in the swamp, Sandy. Time to be up and cracking. I'll do the heavy cracking with the axe down at the water hole. Chopping through that ice is going to be a cold, splashy

23

job. So be nice now and and poke the fire up while I stay warm a little longer."

Sandcherry lay still for a few moments, then crawled out of her sleeping furs and squatted beside the ashes. She pushed the blackened ends of the log stubs together, then knelt and blew on them until they glowed red. By that time Middlehawk was getting into his hunting gear.

Rednecklace sat up, holding the caribou robe around her shoulders.

"Remember that nice guy from Pakwaj, Sandy? The one that gave you the wolverine hood. What was his name . . . something to do with water?"

Sandcherry stopped blowing and looked up. "His name was Waves-break-over-him."

The red coals turned gray. She bowed her head again and renewed the wind pressure. Rednecklace went on.

"That turned out to be a right kind of name. Over on the Kenoshibi something in the long rapid reached up from below and snatched his paddle. That's what he claimed, anyway."

A little flame spurted out in front of Sandcherry's pursed lips and began to climb the dry wood. She leaned back on her heels and replied.

"That was just what happened. Yes, he was a nice guy and he always told the truth. He didn't see anything down there below, but he felt a live force twist that paddle and yank it right out of his hands. He tried to hold it but he couldn't. Then, of course, he struck a rock. He made it to shore, but he was an awful sight. I remember the water running down his jacket and turning pink with blood. And the canoe! There wasn't enough birch bark and cedar left to kindle a fire."

"He got the message, all right," said Rednecklace. "He started walking right from there. Right back into the hills where he came from. He's probably married by this time . . . to somebody with a less magnificent father."

Middlehawk had been clamping his lips together, but he opened them now, spitting out words like stones thrown in anger.

"I didn't kill a one of them! It would have been so easy! And I had every right to. Those thieving carcajous! Coming here and trying to take my daughters away from me!"

He lifted the bearskin that covered the door, then stopped and turned back. The cold air rushed in, making a cloud of steam around him.

"Blackflies on a boggy portage are gentler and more reasonable than women in a winter lodge. I give up. I can't take it any longer. I'm not going to hunt the deer today."

He put down his musket and dropped the powder horn beside it. His daughters, scared now, looked at each other and said nothing.

"I am going to put an end to this abuse and sarcasm. I am going to get you a man."

2

Already several storms had come roaring over the ridge to pile deep drifts in this valley below. Now only the smoke-blackened tip of the wigwam was showing above the snow. Middlehawk climbed the hard-packed ramp to the surface, beat the ice off the toboggan, and dragged it up the path that led to the great stone rampart behind the lodge.

When he reached the summit he talked for a long time with the dark trees. Then he got on the sled and came whizzing back down the trail. The course was crooked, beset by tree-trunks, branches, and boulders. Twisting the high-curved prow to right and to left, dragging first one foot and then the other, muttering defensive charms, he swerved, slewed, and bounded around each menacing obstacle. His snowshoes, hung from his shoulders, swooped and bounced behind him.

When they heard the clatter of those flying frames and the squeal of hardwood on snow, the girls came running out to stand beside the trail. It hadn't taken Rednecklace long to become bold again. She had remembered several qualities that she had always wanted in a husband.

"Bring a young one . . . and good-looking," she shouted.

The father shot past, and she called after him.

"And a good tracker . . . and a sure shot."

He lifted a mittened hand in acknowledgment of the orders.

"And brave."

By that time he was coasting up the far side of the valley. He came to a stop, got off, tied on his snowshoes, and began to pull the toboggan into the piney distance. Sandcherry funneled her hands to her mouth and bellowed.

"If you find two like that, bring them both."

Middlehawk turned and raised his hand again, but this time he swept it down in a gesture of refusal.

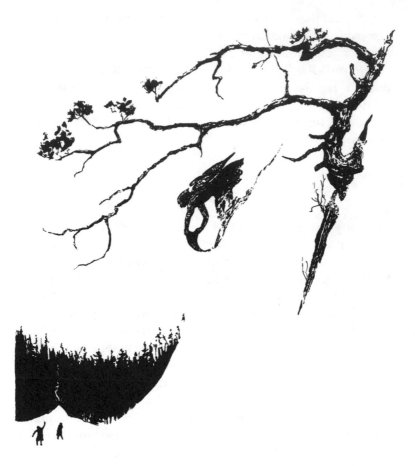

"Now you're asking too much. One man at a time is plenty. Don't imagine that I'm going to give you both away."

He crossed the next range of hills, coasted down into the valley of the Kenoshibi, and followed its icy course upstream around frozen rapids and waterfalls. At noon he stopped where a smaller stream joined the river.

The wind was whipping dry, powdery snow in gusts around him, searching into small openings in his clothing and sawing at his face like flying sand. But he stood for some time, shielding his eyes and speaking in a low, questioning voice while he studied the breaks in the skyline. He must have received an answer, for he turned and followed the lesser waterway. At last he left that ice too. For the rest of the afternoon he pushed along quickly, dragging the toboggan higher and higher into the hills.

The pale sunlight began to fade into darkness. The pointed tops of the evergreens no longer stood out against the sky. The sweat of the day's effort was freezing in his clothing and his toes ached with the cold. He pulled the hood of the parka forward for a little better protection.

He knew that he would not be able to go on much longer, or even to stay alive, without fire and food, but he did not seem worried. And he was not surprised when the bitter wind brought a whiff of burning birch.

He walked into the breeze, stopping at times to sniff. Again he caught the woodsmoke, and with it the rich aroma of roasting moose meat. In a little while he saw light glowing between dark treetrunks.

The snow crunched under his webs as he entered a bright little clearing. A young man straightened up from the cooking fire.

"I am glad that you have come to this camp. Dinner will be ready soon. My name is Pikwak."

"Pikwak. The arrow. No wonder I smelled venison. I am Middlehawk, Doctor of Witchcraft."

"In that case I am especially honored."

He turned back to the fire, raked out red coals, and laid another piece of meat on them.

"Use any of my things that you need, Doctor. I see that you are travelling light."

"That's the way we old timers like it. We're not used to all these white-man gadgets that you young fellows have taken over. My oldest daughter is about your age, and she goes for that stuff too. But I could use a sleeping robe, if you have an extra one."

The slanting roof and sides of a spruce-thatched lean-to had already been covered and made windproof by the blowing snow. In its shelter, Pikwak had prepared a bough bed with one end close to the fire. He spread a blanket of caribou skins over the greenery. Middlehawk sat down on it, took off his mittens, moccasins and foot wrappings, and spread his hands and feet before the heat. The freshly killed meat was tough, but he still had his teeth. He chewed efficiently and happily.

"You must be a good hunter."

27

"The animals are my brothers and my sisters. I respect them and they are often kind to me."

He kicked the fire together, laid a piece of pine stump on it, and squatted beside his guest.

"It is strange that we should meet in this way. I have heard of your remarkable achievements, and of your lovely and accomplished daughters. I grieve for the run of bad luck that has afflicted their suitors. But there is a bright side to those sad accidents. The young ladies are still there.

"I had been thinking of coming down to call on you when the Kenoshibi opens. How would you feel about that, Doctor?"

"To tell you the truth, I was just thinking along those lines myself. But the breakup is still months away. Perhaps an earlier visit could be arranged."

When all the cooked meat was gone Middlehawk asked for the liver. He cut off and ate several slices. Then he wrapped himself in the robe and lay back, pretending to sleep. Pikwak brought in boughs for his own bed, banked the fire, and rolled up in another skin blanket, taking with him a little birch bark and kindling to keep dry for the morning.

After a while, the old man heard a gentle snore. He sat up, opened his medicine bundle, and took out a hawk's foot, a dried toad, and several unidentifiable objects. He closed his eyes. His hands moved, and so did his lips, but no words came. None, at least, that a human ear could hear.

An hour passed. The fire burned low. The doctor opened his eyes a little and saw that the lower part of Pikwak's robe, where his feet had been, was empty.

He stirred the coals, put on fresh wood, and continued to develop his enchantment. He was speaking loudly now, but his victim, held in the grip of the magic, did not wake. When the sky became light again behind the treetops he had shrunk to the size of a little boy and had a child's round face and slender body. Middlehawk picked him up, wrapped as he was in fur, and carried him to the toboggan.

The compressed track had frozen hard, making a good trail for the return trip. Much of the way the doctor just sat on the sled, holding the sleeping boy before him and steering with skillful ease, while they coasted down from the high country.

3

Middlehawk left his captive at the edge of the home clearing, eased himself down to the entry of the lodge and walked in. The sisters looked up, their eyes bright.

Rednecklace was the first to speak.

"Did you bring him?"

"Of course I brought him. I always keep my word. He's out on the toboggan at the end of the trail. Whichever one of you touches him first can have him."

The girls didn't stop to put on their moccasins. Sandcherry tore down the bearskin getting out the door. She was in the lead at that point, but she slipped as she climbed the grade. Rednecklace caught her skirt, pulled her back, and scrambled up ahead of her.

Middlehawk sat down beside the fire, fished out a glowing coal, and lit his pipe. He was relaxed and ready when Rednecklace came storming back.

"You disgusting old swindler! He's nothing but a droopy-drawers kid! His nose is even dribbling."

Her father looked up at her sadly and blew a reproachful stream of smoke through his own long and craggy nose.

"I am very tired. It was a long, cold walk. I was up all night catching that man for you. And this is how you express your thanks. An ungrateful child is sharper than a lynx's claw."

Sandcherry carried the boy in, laid him, still sleeping, on the balsam greenery and covered him with a robe. She stamped her feet but that didn't get all the snow out from between her toes so she reached down and cleared them with her fingers. Then she straightened up and turned to Middlehawk.

"Why did you bring us a little squirt like this?"

"Your sister asked for a young one."

"I said a young man. You know perfectly well that I didn't mean a child!"

"He's young and handsome. You can see that. I also made sure that he is brave and a good hunter. You'll have to take my word on those qualities for the present. But as soon as he's old enough, he'll bring in the meat.

"You loaded me with specifications. I met every one of them. And you still complain."

"What am I supposed to do for a husband?"

"I guess you'll have to wait until he grows up. You can marry him then."

Before a month had passed, the father began to regret that promise. Rednecklace quickly became fond of the little fiance, and so did Sandcherry. He spoke of them as his aunts, and called Middlehawk grandfather. The sisters combed and greased his hair, mended his small cuts and bruises, told him scary old stories to make him behave, and made him wash his face every day and take a bath in the sweat lodge at least once a week.

They fed him well as long as the meat lasted. When the snow deepened in the late winter, game became scarce. Not even the sorcerer's magic could create deer where there were none. But even then the sisters made sure that Pikwak got his share of whatever small creatures they were able to snare, and of the wild rice, roots, and dried berries they had stored. Plus a little extra to grow on.

And grow he did. That was the worst part of it. Middlehawk had been confident that his witchery, applied regularly and at close range, would keep Pikwak a permanent child. But already he was noticeably taller, and filling out, too. And growing up in other ways. When the aunties hugged him, he hugged back with more enthusiasm than a little nephew should, and sometimes his hands found their way into intimate places and lingered there until they were evicted. Rednecklace and Sandcherry screamed with laughter at these innocent aggressions and retaliated with playful slaps, but Middlehawk did not join in the merriment.

The doctor sensed that there was more to this development than the loving care that his daughters were providing. Another power was working against his magic.

When Pikwak had been older, he had been something of a magician himself. Not a professional like Middlehawk, but handy with small charms, able to control the weather to some extent, and influential with trees, stones, and animals.

Once Sandcherry saw him looking up into an aspen and talking. When she sneaked closer she could see a porcupine in the branches above him. Pikwak would say a few words and apparently would get some kind of an answer. After a while the porcupine came rattling down the trunk and they walked off together, chatting.

The boy couldn't remember anything of life before his long sleep, but he seemed to understand how a man should do things. He paddled as though he were part of the canoe. He could follow tracks like a young wolf. He made himself a short, strong bow, and kept the family supplied with squirrels, grouse, and big, long-legged hares. These manly skills added to the doctor's worries. Was there no way to stop the rush to maturity? Well, there would be one way.

On a calm evening he climbed the trail to the ridge. He didn't take his drum. That would have been a giveaway. He just sat down on the rock—the naked bedrock that curved swiftly down to the the edge of the cliff and then dropped straight and sheer into 'Tschgumi's clear water. And there he talked to his friends and partners, the spruce.

The black spruce of the subarctic forest is not like the tidy cone-shaped Christmas-tree spruce that you plant on lawns. It is a wild, shaggy thing that shoots out crooked branches this way and that way, and forks its trunk if it feels like it. It has a bad reputation as a collaborator in magic.

These dark trees knew well that they had no right to be up here, so far from the muskeg. They had massacred the pines that used to stand on this side of the ridge. Since then they had been quarreling among themselves, sending raiding roots into each other's territory. By this time they were starved for earth-sustenance and deformed by the gales of the great lake. They were hunch-backs whose crooked trunks grew slanting away from the force of the prevailing winds. Their lower branches, festooned with the dangling, wispy moss known as old man's beard, ran far out over the stone. Their painfully knotted roots poked into every crevice, searching eagerly for a little life-giving dirt.

They could never have survived in this place without sorcery. They had to work with the witch doctor and he had to work with them. But they were willing accomplices, always eager to bring disaster on helpless humans.

So when he had talked with them only a short time they began to sigh and wave their branches. Soon an evil spirit came crawling up the precipice, dripping cold water and even colder wickedness so that it left a dark smear on the rocks behind it.

This was a water-manedo, an old friend of Middlehawk's. The sorcerer welcomed it and offered it a lighted pipe. The horrible creature goggled its fish eyes and took a long pull, drawing in its scaly cheeks and letting the smoke filter slowly out through its gills. Then it passed the pipe back to its host.

When they had sat for the proper period, silent and motionless except for this exchange, Middlehawk told of his problem and outlined the solution he had in mind.

The monster puffed for a while in sinister silence. Then it took the pipe out of its mouth and spoke.

"Seems a little rough on the kid, doesn't it?"

"He's brought it on himself. I know witchcraft when I see it, and this growth is sorcerous. The nasty brat is magically sprouting, stretching himself out. He is also beginning to smell like a man. At the same time he's casting a spell on my little girls. If he's not stopped now he's going to steal one or the other of them. And that would break my heart."

"Well, Doc, I suppose we should take care of him for you. Seeing that it's you. Only don't forget it when you make the next sacrifice. I don't want to make a big issue of it, but that last dog was not up to your usual standard."

"The next one will be as white as new snow and as fat as a bear in the autumn."

The manedo sucked thoughtfully on the pipe stem. "I don't really like being a party to this kind of a deal. But I stand by my friends. And I do have a weakness for fat dogs."

It gave Middlehawk certain instructions. Then it wriggled down the rocks and plopped back into the lake.

4

As soon as the river ice broke, Middlehawk invited his adopted grandson for a fishing trip. They crossed the hills and walked up the bank of the Kenoshibi to the long rapids.

"The suckers and the jackfish-pike are running," said the doctor, "and here's the place where you're going to get a really big one." He handed the boy a three-pronged fish spear. "Wade right out there. The water may feel a little cold until you get used to it. But you can't let that bother you if you are to be a fisherman. Just keep harpooning fish and tossing them to me. We'll soon fill this basket. And watch for that big one."

Pikwak splashed in. It was cold all right. Any colder and it would be frozen. And the current was powerful. He had to brace himself with the spear to keep his footing. But he went on, working his way between the boulders and over the stony bottom. He didn't want to give up in front of Grandfather Middlehawk.

The fish were all around him, swimming strong against the current. He could feel them bumping his legs. But the river was pushing him so hard that every time he went to lift the spear he had to set it quickly back against the rocks and lean on the handle to keep from being swept away.

Suddenly there was a terrifying commotion in the water downstream. An enormous jackfish surged up out of the river, opened a mouth full of hooked-back, one-way teeth, and spoke to him.

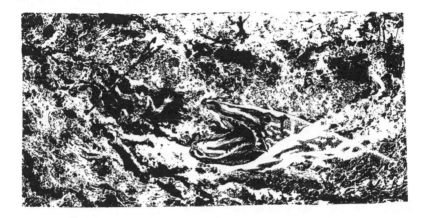

"You are looking for fish?"

Pikwak's mouth hung open but he said nothing.

"I heard that you want to catch some fish to eat. Well here I am, you can start on me. . . . All right, then I'll eat you instead. But what are you doing with that spear?

"I was just leaning on it," said Pikwak. "I haven't injured any of your relatives."

"Well, how can I eat you when you have a sharp thing like that in your hand? Throw it away before you hurt somebody with it."

There was a shout from the shore.

"That's the big one, grandson. Don't let him get away. Stick it to him!"

Pikwak lifted the spear from its purchase on the bottom. Nobody could tell whether he intended to throw it away or to stab with it, because instantly the river rolled him over, snatched the weapon out of his hand, and swept him into the fish's mouth. The fish swallowed, but carefully, not chewing. The boy slid down a slippery passageway and came to rest in a somewhat wider cavern.

He began to shout.

"Dear Uncle Jackfish-pike. Men and fish should be friends. Please let me out."

"You didn't look very fish-friendly with that spear," hissed the jackfish. "And in any case I can't let you out here where we are being watched and maybe listened to. You wouldn't want to get me in wrong with the manedo, would you? So quiet down and I'll see what I can do about it."

It was dark and cold in that fish's belly. Pikwak lay still, without saying another word. He could hear the rippling and roaring of water beside and above. He knew that they were travelling at high speed but he had no idea in what direction.

After a while the motion stopped, light came flooding in, and he heard the jackfish call, "End of the voyage. Everybody out. This is as close as I can get to your place."

Pikwak squirmed up the gullet and peeked between the open jaws. He could see boulders close, and trees beyond them. He crawled carefully over the big, curved teeth, splashed ashore, and found himself on the beach of the cove below the Middle-hawk lodge.

The jackfish called after him, "Send the women down here with baskets. They will find something they'll like."

He scraped back off the pebbles, finned into deeper water, submerged, then surfaced again.

"Just remember, in case anybody asks, that you were kicking so hard and making such a nuisance of yourself that I had no choice but to toss you out. And you don't need to mention that I took you to shore."

"I'll keep that in mind, uncle. You were not to blame. I am ashamed to have been so obnoxious a dinner. In no way could you have digested me. And I had to swim a long way to get back here."

He walked up to the wigwam. His aunts looked at him in astonishment. Rednecklace put her hand on the top of his head and pushed down as though she expected that something inside him would give way.

"How did you get tall so quickly?"

"He's grown the length of a man's foot since he left us this morning," said Sandcherry. "A big man's."

"Yes, well never mind that," replied Pikwak, "there is work to be done. Take your two biggest baskets and go down to the beach and bring back what you find there."

As soon as they had gone he stood beside the cross-pole that was fastened above the fire. Last night he had reached up to hang a kettle from it. He could see over it now.

Soon the sisters came staggering back, bent under heavy loads and grinning broadly. The baskets, slung by straps on their backs, were full of fresh fish. Rednecklace called to him as they entered the clearing.

"That's the best day's catch we ever saw. How did you do it?"

"You wouldn't understand. Just cut them and dry them."

The women spent the rest of the day splitting the fish and hanging them over a slow fire. Their hands moved fast. Long lines of pale slabs hung from a rack of birch poles when, late in the afternoon, their father came down the trail. He was stepping along at a sprightly gait, almost prancing, you might say, and grinning broadly.

"I am weighed down by the heavy news that I must bring you. A terrible accident happened at the rapids today."

Just then Pikwak appeared from the other side of the clearing, his face poking out from under a load of firewood. The doctor's eyes widened and his mouth sagged at the corners, but he gave no other sign of surprise.

"Where is that big jackfish?"

Pikwak slipped the tump strap from his head, dropping the wood beside the fire.

"He got away."

"I warned you not to let that happen. And what did you do with my spear?"

"I lost it."

"You're getting to be a big boy now. You'll have to learn to be more responsible about taking care of valuable equipment. I gave the white man two beaver skins for that iron spear head."

"You paid too much for it, grandfather. Those guys will take you every time. But yes, I'll be more careful from now on. For sure I will."

After that Middlehawk went every day to talk with the spruces. He took his drum with him and he didn't care who knew it. When the wind was right they could hear the thumping and chanting loud in the wigwam. The sisters looked at each other and at Pikwak. But he didn't seem to be worried.

35

The forest warmed under the berry moon. The valley was aromatic with the smell of spruce and pine. The waters of the Kenoshibi subsided and mother ducks led downy broods across its surface.

One night when the old man had finished his chowder he belched politely, lifted the lid of the kettle, and looked down into it.

"That fish stew is very nice and there seems to be plenty of it left. But now I think I'd like a change. Let's you and I go to the island tomorrow, grandson, and get some eggs."

Before Pikwak could answer, Rednecklace broke in loudly. "Oh no. It's too late to gather eggs. By this time, each one will have a growing gull in it."

"Daughter, that's what I've been waiting for. You don't know what's good."

"The blueberries on the south side of the burn are almost ripe," said Sandcherry. "That will give you a change in diet. We have no need for eggs."

5

A few days later the women left before daylight, loaded with kettles and bark boxes for berries. As soon as they were out of sight, Middlehawk said that this would be a good day to gather gull eggs.

They carried the canoe down to the shore. A heavy mist hung low. Pikwak could just make out dim treetops as they passed the point at the mouth of the cove, and soon these disappeared. He heard a rippling sound from under the bow, as it drove through the still water.

When the sun came out he looked back. The hills were only a faint strip far behind them. Ahead he could see nothing but the curved line where the sky met the lake. They'd be in bad shape if a storm were to come up now. But no wind would be likely to blow while the doctor was on the water.

After a while the horizon was broken by a dot that grew steadily larger, and finally became a stone island. On one side, a pile of boulders supported a clump of blueberry bushes and a twisted little spruce. The other end tailed off into a point of shattered rock. Pikwak could see that this was a sacred place.

As they approached it, Middlehawk slowed his paddling and began a chant. A tornado of gulls whipped up from the rocks and swirled overhead. He stopped the boat beside a flat table of stone.

"Get out here, grandson. You will find that the spaces between the rocks are crowded with nests. Take this bag and fill it with eggs. Don't break any of them. And leave your paddle in the canoe, so that you won't lose it as you did the spear."

Pikwak stepped carefully out. The rocks were slippery with droppings and white with feathers. Nests were everywhere. The gulls soared angrily around him, making passes at his head as he picked up the eggs. He knew that they would not attack him while the wabeno continued his soothing song.

When the bag was full he turned back toward the landing. The canoe was no longer there. Middlehawk had stroked it out into the lake.

And now his tune changed. The chant became loud and rasping.

"Gulls of 'Tschgumi. I give you this thief. He has defiled your island and stolen your eggs. He has an evil character but he is young, tender and delicious. And he's all yours now. Tear him to pieces and eat every bit of him."

He turned the canoe and, with quick strokes, set it speeding back toward the unseen mainland.

The gulls screamed a war cry as they closed in, banking and wheeling in narrowing circles around their captive.

"I'll take the first taste," cried a gray gull, diving at the boy. But a big white bird shouldered him off.

"I am the ogema, your leader. I will be the first to strike this enemy." He darted in and snipped a bite out of Pikwak's ear. A trickle of blood ran down the boy's cheek and dripped on his chest.

He held up the bag where they could all see it.

"Wait a little, brothers and sisters," he shouted. "Wait, or these eggs might get broken. They are the future of your tribe. Willingly I give them back to you. I have handled them with loving care. You will find that not one of them is cracked or missing."

"Don't even listen to him," shrieked the gray. "Tear him up and eat him as the witchman told us. Let him break the eggs! The women can lay more."

"That's easy for you to say," screamed the hen gulls. "Save the eggs!"

Circling thoughtfully, the big white gull swallowed his piece of Pikwak then called out his opinion.

"He isn't really that wonderful. I like fish better."

"Then that settles that," said the boy. "You know how old ones are when they get bragging about their grandchildren. I never claimed to be such great eating." He put the sack down very gently. Between his feet.

"But, brothers and sisters, we still have a problem to work out together. I've enjoyed my stay on your lovely island. Now I must leave you. I ask you, my dear new friends, to carry me home."

"That's out of the question," said the white gull. "I'm the biggest and strongest bird here, as well as the wisest and the most handsome. But I couldn't possibly lift you. You'll have to swim for it."

"Oh, the water is too cold for swimming. And I'm just a little boy. Come now, all get together beneath me and you will lift me like a feather."

He leaned forward and spread his arms.

"Well, we'll give it a try," said the ogema. "But we won't be responsible in case you drop and are damaged."

He squawked out a call to the others.

"You heard what the man said. Get under him and get lifting."

Swiftly they gathered beneath him, pushing up on his body, his legs, and his arms. With a great screaming and flapping of wings they got him off the rocks.

The ogema, flying close to the mass of birds but a little outside them, supervised and gave orders. He had followed the white man's ships for the garbage they threw overboard, and along with those morsels he had picked up some of their way of talking.

"Come on, you lazy buggers! Get your backs into it."

He began to sing a wierd white-man chant. The wings beat in time to the song, and bore the boy higher.

The gray gull was working hard, but he was still angry.

"Some feather!" he screeched.

"Which way?" the ogema called.

Pikwak didn't dare move his arm, but he pointed with one finger. The flock swept off in that direction.

Through the flapping wings he could get glimpses of the waves below. After a while he saw Middlehawk. The old man was trailing his paddle with one hand. With the other he was shading his eyes from the sun. He was looking up, trying to make out what was passing over.

The ogema peeled off from the flock and plunged straight down at him. At the last moment he pulled out of the dive and curved upwards. There was a loud splat, and a stream of white gull manure ran down the doctor's face.

6

As soon as he had been lifted off the island, Pikwak had begun to grow rapidly. The gull-mass sagged under him. The ogema saw, flew in underneath, and added his own wing-power to the hoist. But soon even this combination began to lose altitude.

"There's something wrong with this son of a buck," gasped the leader. "He's getting heavier every minute."

"Hang on just a little longer," squealed the gray gull. "We're almost there."

"Make up your mind, grayback!" screamed the others. "You're the one wanted to eat him. He's getting too much for us."

They were approaching the shore, but slanting down fast. One of the gulls gave up and swung away, and then another. Those that were left could no longer hold the boy up. They rose in a spreading cloud above him.

He fell, flapping like a bird without feathers, struck with a stupendous splash, and plummeted deep in a reverse rocket of bubbles.

'Tschgumi is icy cold, even in summer, and is inhabited by any number of dangerous spirits. Way down there, far beneath its surface, Pikwak was struggling. He seemed to hang, suspended in the depths, for long moments, arms and legs churning. Then he began to rise, slowly at first but gaining momentum. Just when he thought that he wouldn't be able to hold his breath for another second, he bobbed up to the surface.

The ogema circled once above him.

"You're on your own now, brother. I hope you make it. I'm not going to bet on it, though."

Then he flew away after the others.

Pikwak struck out hard. He knew that he would have to move fast, both to keep his circulation strong and to hold his body parallel to the surface in the thin upper level of water where the chill had been eased a little by the sun. Sometimes he slowed, so that his legs began to sink, but then the quick cold spurred him, and the thought of the terrible things that would be watching him from below.

At last, as he flailed blindly ahead, his knee struck hard on a submerged rock. The hurt brought joy. He was getting close.

He was numb and completely exhausted as he drew himself out of the water and climbed up the slippery boulders that guarded the land from the lake's rage. He crawled over many other stones, reached a level, mossy spot, and slept heavily.

Then came the long walk down the corridor between the forest and the water. Here he had to work his way around or over barriers of stones and driftwood that repeatedly blocked his progress. He was limping from his bruised knee.

At evening he stumbled up the trail from the cove to the lodge. Rednecklace was cooking. Sandcherry was laying out strips of birch bark to keep the night damps off an expanse of berries that had been spread on mats to dry. Middlehawk, sitting before the lodge, was the first to see him.

"Where are the eggs?"

"I gave them back to the gulls."

"To waste good food is a sin that brings its own punishment. Before winter we shall be hungry. Remember that, boy."

"I will make meat for you, grandfather."

"See how he's grown," said Rednecklace. "He's quite caught up to you, Sandy. And hear how his voice has changed. He has aged five years since we left camp this morning."

She paused and then went on.

"Tonight he's old enough for marriage. And so am I. It's time that I become his wife."

"Oh no it isn't," shouted Sandcherry. "He'd rather have me, wouldn't you, Pikwak?"

"I'm very grateful to you, Auntie Sandcherry. And to you also, my dear Aunt Rednecklace. Together you have cared for me for all these months since I was a little child. Let us continue together. I would be happy and honored to marry you both."

"You certainly can't do any such thing," said Middlehawk. "Not in these modern times. That good and holy man, the white black-robe, has made it clear that no Indian is now allowed to have more than one wife."

"Well now I've heard everything," said Rednecklace. "The great witch doctor has told us, every time we've ever visited the settlement, that the only good white men are the quiet ones out in the cemetery. And here he comes to us quoting their medicine man and promoting their outlandish marriage customs!"

Indignation overcame her powers of speech and she chattered like an angry squirrel. But Sandcherry came in loud and firm.

"That one-wife idea is well enough for those fat ladies down south at the settlement, white and Indian both, that don't have to do anything but sleep and eat and bat away flies. Every lodge up here in the north, as you yourself told us, father, needs two good women. Besides, these accidents keep happening to our men."

"Don't be in such a sweat," said Middlehawk. "In the first place you should both be ashamed of wanting to rob the cradle-board. Also, this great hunter of yours is all right on rabbits and shows no fear of chipmunks, but I don't know how he'll do with big game. He dropped my valuable spear in the river, he let the big fish get away and he left the eggs on the island. I doubt that so improvident a man can support one wife, let alone two hearty eaters like you.

"As you know, though, I am always reasonable. So I tell you what we'll do. Wait until the first snow falls. The first good tracking snow. Then he and I will go hunting together. If he makes some real meat, you can do what you please about marriage."

"Oh sure," said Rednecklace. "If he makes meat and if nothing happens to him out there alone in the woods with you."

"Grandfather is right," said Pikwak. "He is concerned for your future. I can understand that. We will go hunting together in the snow. There I will show him what a good provider I'll be for his daughters."

7

Summer cooled. The birch and aspen leaves turned yellow. Middlehawk and his people paddled and portaged up the Kenoshibi to a little lake, a deep pocket, in the hills of glacial stone. In that quiet water, slim stems curved under the weight of the wild rice.

Another family arrived at the same time. Together they gathered and processed the grain. In the evenings and at dawn Pikwak hunted the fat ducks that were also working on the harvest. Soon the stalks rustled empty in the breeze and the only kernels left were those that had sunk into the muddy bottom to seed next year's crop.

The two families held a feast of thanksgiving to the spirits of rice and duck. Prayers were made that the moose and caribou also would be kind during the coming winter so that all the people present might live to meet here when leaves became bright-colored again.

By the time they got back to the home lodge the lake winds had blown the trees bare. The nights were getting long and in the mornings the women had to break thin ice to get water. Pikwak made himself a stout bow of hickory and reinforced it with sinew.

Middlehawk's drum throbbed from the ridge, the sound rising and falling with the shifting winds. Whenever it stopped, Rednecklace worried.

"The new rice is good and there is still plenty of fish, but soon we must have fat against the cold. He should be making meat medicine but he is quiet too often for that. I fear that he is doing business with some evil spirit. Don't go hunting with him, Pikwak."

One morning the earth was covered with a heavy carpet of snow.

"This will be just right for moose," said Middlehawk. "And it's not so deep that we'll need snowshoes. Come, grandson. We will walk up into the hills and find the trail of a nice young cow."

He shouldered his musket and Pikwak took up his new bow, ignoring Rednecklace's entreaties.

They walked all day but didn't see the track of a moose nor of any other deer, nor even of a rabbit. As dusk closed in, the doctor stopped beside a steep rock outcropping. An egg-shaped boulder, as big as a small wigwam, had evidently fallen from this height and lay a little way from its base.

"The wind is turning cold. We will camp here where we will be well sheltered. Make the fire beside that round stone and it will reflect the heat back on us. Bring in plenty of wood."

He set up a framework of poles running out a little from the face of the cliff, braced it firmly, and thatched it with spruce boughs. Pikwak built the fire and got more boughs for bedding.

"We will have to go to bed without supper, grandson. But you must accustom yourself to that if you are to become a hunter."

Pikwak understood all that and was loosening his clothes for sleep. He took off his damp moccasins.

"Here, give me those," said Middlehawk. "I will hang them by the fire. In the morning they will be dry and warm for you. Tomorrow we will go on until we get a moose or a caribou and then we will eat. Now sleep well and don't bother about the fire. I'll take care of it."

The old man was as good as his word. The temperature dropped during the night but Pikwak slept soundly. He woke just before daylight. The stone egg shone in the light of flames rising cheerfully around a fresh log.

He got up and took his moccasins from the sticks on which the doctor had hung them. They were dry and warm all right but when he put them on, his feet pushed through the soles. He turned quickly to look at Middlehawk, and caught him peeking through partly open eyes.

"That rascal wind!" exclaimed the old man. "It blew the flame against your shoes and scorched out the bottoms."

"I see that yours are all right, grandfather."

"Yes, your behavior must have offended a wind-manedo. They are strict. They won't stand for a lot of fooling around.

They're fair, though. This one respected my property. And that's a good thing for both of us. I'll go on now, kill whatever kind of deer I find first, and hurry back to you with meat and hide. Then I will make you new moccasins."

He put on the shoes, picked up his musket, and started off across the snow. Then he stopped and called back.

"It may take me a while. If you happen to get hungry while you're waiting you can eat your uppers. But be sure to boil them until they're tender. Otherwise they won't be very good."

He strode off into the woods. Pikwak thought that he might as well wait here for summer as for that old man to bring meat or moccasins.

He took a few tentative barefoot steps toward the lake and the home lodge. A few were plenty. He hurried back to the warm earth beside the fire.

The flame was burning low, but the big stone still glowed red. It would hold the heat for many hours. Pikwak stood watching it, thinking. Then he began to talk to it.

"Brother boulder, your good heat warms me. I am sure that you would not willingly stand there and watch me die in the cold. Roll then down those tracks whose heels point toward the south. Melt me a path through the snow that I may return to the lodge of the kind women who have cared for me and who have promised to be my wives. Their fish and rice soup will taste good tonight."

The stone moved a little. It broke away from the frozen grip of the earth, as a loaded toboggan, that has settled into ice, breaks loose under the combined effort of men, women, and dogs. It rolled down the trail, slowly at first, then speeding up to a good walking gait. The snow melted under it leaving a path of dry leaves, earth, and moss. Pikwak followed close, ready to urge it on if it should falter or to shout a correction in case it headed off in a wrong direction.

But it seemed to know the way, or else was able to see the tracks, for it followed every turn. Sometimes it slowed on the uphill grades and occasionally it grunted with the strain, but each time it reached the summit and rolled down the other side, bounding over the rocky places. On those falling-away slopes the man had to run to keep up with it.

At mid-afternoon, as it rolled down a gentle slant, the stone slowed quickly and stopped. Pikwak came running up behind it.

"Not here, brother. The lodge is still far away. Oh, do not stop here."

The boulder did not answer, but Pikwak thought he heard a sound coming from it. A sound like a dog blowing out through his nose to clear it for taking in a scent. The stone was trembling a little but paying no attention to his orders and pleas.

Suddenly the boulder went rolling off at an angle to the trail. Pikwak watched in dismay. It wheeled in a great circle, crashing through brush, snapping off small trees and changing course to pass around big ones. Soon it came charging back and stopped again.

All night that big piece of granite had stood by the fire, getting hotter and hotter, but still it had not cracked. Now, after all this time, there was a loud report. A fragment flew off, soared high, curved in glowing flight, and crashed down into a pile of fallen timber at the center of its circle.

There was an angry bellow and the mass heaved up in an eruption of treetrunks, stones, and rubble, followed by the head of a bear. His little red eyes winked, squinted, and came into focus on Pikwak.

8

"This is only the moon when the rivers freeze," roared the bear, "and I can't have been sleeping for more than a week. And here you come dropping hot rocks on me!"

Pikwak bowed his head.

"Oh gracious, kind, and hairy uncle," he said. "Forgive me and my brother, the stone, for disturbing you in your house under the snow. But I feel great happiness on meeting you at this important moment. My aunties, my grandfather, and I have been living on fish, rice, and berries for a long time. We crave fat."

"So you waked me out of my lovely sleep to complain about your grub. And such good stuff, at that. Fish and berries are my favorite fodder. I'm not really hungry, but do you happen to have any of them with you?"

"No, great black one. I have eaten nothing since yesterday morning. And now the cold hand of winter is squeezing us. If we don't get some good fat meat we will starve and freeze."

"Well, that's your problem. I'm going back to bed."

"Ah, but it is your problem, also, dear uncle, as I shall explain. We animals, and the plants too, are all in this battered world together. We each must feed on others in order to survive. And, to each of us, old Pauguk, death, comes in time. Now he has come for you. To feed myself and my hungry family it is necessary that I kill you.

"But do not be alarmed. I give you my word that you will receive every honor. I will not allow any woman to eat of your heart, hand, or nose. I will treat your bones with deep respect. And I will paint your skull with a broad band and fasten it high in a tree. Your spirit will be proud."

"Thanks," said the bear. "Such piety is heartening in this age of skepticism. Offhand, I'd say that your logic appears sound. But I'll need more time to consider the interesting philosophical points that you have raised. Let's get together again some time soon and discuss them further. It's been a real pleasure to meet such an understanding person. Have a nice day."

He turned and took off in a bouncing, flat-footed gallop over the snow and through the brush. Pikwak notched an arrow and drew the powerful bow. As the bear approached the path that had been cleared by the stone, the bowstring twanged. The black uncle fell across the melted trail.

For all his talk, he hadn't really run very fast. He must have felt sorry for the hungry people.

Pikwak stood beside the sprawling mass of the carcass and said the ceremonial words of thanks with real gratitude. Then he swiftly skinned and dressed the bear, talking to it as he worked. He was already chewing sweet pieces of fat, so his words may have been a little garbled, but the bear spirit would understand.

He wrapped the heart, paws, liver, nose, and solid sections of loin, belly fat, and hindquarter in the hide. From the entrails he drew out the long intestine and carefully cleaned it.

He squatted there for a while, assembling his thoughts and fears. Then he took the end of the gut in his hand and spoke into it with reverence.

"Tell me, black owner of the forest, will the grandfather return as he promised to bring help for me?"

He put the tube to his ear and listened.

"That is as I thought. What will he do next and how can I protect myself from him and obtain my aunties in marriage?"

He listened again, nodding occasionally.

"Thank you, kind hairy one, for the fat meat and for the wise counsel. I will do exactly as you advise."

He slung the bundle on his back from a strap across his head and turned to the stone egg, which had been resting in the trail.

"Now, brother, it is time for us to continue."

The boulder groaned a little and began to rock back and forth, then rolled down the trail, slowly accelerating. It did not stop again until it came to rest before the wigwam.

The doctor was eating fish as Pikwak entered. His jaws stopped working and his face was wracked by a spasm of despair. Rednecklace looked up in alarm, then jumped to her feet.

"A bone in your throat, father?"

He did not answer. She struck him hard on the back. He gasped and coughed. Then he put a finger into his mouth and seemed to take something out, glance at it, and throw it aside.

"Thank you, my daughter. Yes, it was a fish bone, but I'm all right now. And I am happy to see you, grandson. I had intended, as soon as dinner was finished, to have the girls make you a pair of moccasins. I would have started at dawn to carry them to you."

"You are kind, grandfather, to come so quickly to my assistance. And I have brought you a present. A bride-gift. The rest of this black one is also yours. The women can bring that in tomorrow."

He placed the bundle of bear, with formal precision, before the old man.

"And now I have the honor to ask you for your daughters in marriage."

Middlehawk hudged violently backwards as though repulsed by the shaggy offering.

"Don't touch it!" he screamed.

But Rednecklace had already cut the binding. She and Sandcherry plunged their hands into the dripping contents.

"Don't bite the heart or the paws!" shouted Pikwak. "Or the nose either."

"Stop hollering at us, both of you," mumbled Rednecklace, her mouth already full. "We know the rules. You must think we're a couple of slobs."

"You can have the insides and the feet," said Sandcherry. "And the snoot, too. This is what we want. This first, Pikwak, and then you." She stuffed a big blob of fat into her mouth and neither sister spoke again for a long time.

"Oh, well," said Middlehawk, "marry in haste and repent at leisure."

He snatched up the belly section, sank his teeth into it, drew his long knife and slashed and sawed the big mouthful off, taking care, however, not to cut his nose.

When the fat-hunger had been satisfied, the hindquarter was hung over the fire to roast for the wedding feast.

9

Next day the women followed the trail to the carcass, completed the butchering, and carried in the meat. They rendered the fat into a rich white lard that filled many bark boxes. As soon as they had finished with the bear they hurried out to take care of a moose that Pikwak had brought down. He seemed to have no trouble finding game when he went alone.

"We've got to give you credit," Sandcherry said to Middlehawk. "You brought us a good hunter all right. We won't be gnawing old bones this winter."

"We might have other troubles, though," said Rednecklace. "I heard that drum of yours, father, as we came in with the last load of moose meat. You were up on the ridge talking to the manedog again.

"So now you must understand this: you can stay in my wigwam . . ."

"Our wigwam," interrupted Sandcherry. "I helped you build it. It's mine as much as it is yours."

"All right then," Rednecklace went on. "You can stay in our wigwam and we will feed you. But no more of your tricks. From now on you must let our husband alone."

Middlehawk looked at her as though she had stabbed him, but his mouth was too full of moose to answer.

The inland lakes and rivers froze, and later 'Tschgumi, for several miles from the shore, although farther out he remained open. Two caribou and another moose hung beside the wigwam. It was too cold on the ridge for talking or drumming. The family relaxed. Maybe the doctor had relented.

On a gray morning he sat hunched, looking out from under his protruding eyebrows at little wisps of snow that whirled down from the smokehole and hissed into the fire. Rednecklace was dressing Pikwak's hair, working a handful of fat into each side of his head.

The air was rich with the odors of grease, woodsmoke, and curing hides, and with the warm fragrance of hard-working people who live together in a small space where all the wash-water must be hacked out of ice and carried through deep snow. Middlehawk's voice, when he spoke, was as comfortable and friendly as those familiar old smells.

"Today, son-in-law, I will introduce you to a sport that will be appropriate to one so recently emerged from childhood. You and I will go tobogganing."

Rednecklace stopped the massage.

"Not on the spruce ridge. Not in all those stumps and boulders and jackpines."

"That is where the speed is," said Middlehawk. "Your brave man wouldn't be satisfied with any slow course. And such a skillful fellow will have no difficulty. There is a good trail between and around those small obstacles. All he will have to do will be to turn the sled from time to time."

"I'd like that," said Pikwak. "I take it that you will make the same run when I finish?"

"Oh, certainly," replied Middlehawk. "Yes. Of course, yes. Just as soon as you're completely finished."

"Then comb and tie my hair, wife. After that your father and I will rise and go."

Rednecklace strung out the job for a long time while the sisters objected loudly. But when the head was sleek and shining-smooth and there was nothing more to say that hadn't been said several times already, the two men walked off together, Pikwak pulling the toboggan. While they climbed the zigzag trail, Rednecklace waited at its foot with bandages, balsam balm, and cedar splints. Sandcherry stationed herself about half way down in case, as she thought likely, that should be as far as the run went.

At the summit, a cold wind from 'Tschgumi was flogging the spruce trees. It drove icy snowflakes against Pikwak's face, but he could see, far below, the new, black ice on the great lake. Long, shifting drifts of snow were wriggling across it like white snakes.

He turned and looked back toward the lodge. The trail down was steeper, and more crooked and dangerous, than he had thought. But he placed the toboggan at its start, seated himself upon it, and started to push off.

"Hold on," said Middlehawk, "you're taking the wrong run. Here, I'll help you."

He spun the sled around, grabbed the young man's shoulders, and gave him a mighty shove down the sharp slope toward the cliff.

"Steer well, son-in-law!" he shouted. "Fly far, Arrow!"

A misty blizzard of driving snow. The scream of the frozen crust beneath. Blurred forms of trees whizzing by. Ahead the end of the white carpet approaching at deadly speed. Beyond that, the great darkness.

"Spruce, spruce, little black spruce on the edge, stretch out your arms and save me."

Branches whipping in the wind.

Slap! Slap!

A splintering explosion. The tree's fingers have him. The shock almost tears the wood apart. The spruce cracks, shrieks with pain. But it holds tight. To the man and the toboggan with its branches and to the rock with its roots.

"Hang on, my dear boy! I'm coming," shouted the doctor. He started down the slope but his moccasins skidded on the icy surface. He stopped, clinging to a tree.

"Don't bother, father-in-law." Pikwak called back. "Please, just don't come near me. I'm doing all right."

He had tied the toboggan line around his waist while the spruce held him. Now he took hold of the branch and worked his way up it, hand over hand, through the needles and frozen moss to the trunk. Out along other branches beyond it until he was able to get a little footing. The next tree reached a hand down to help him.

Several times his feet almost spun out from under him. Again he staggered under the impact of a sudden gust of wind. But he kept a grip on the tough and springy spruce.

Up the slope from tree to tree. Taking firm hold on one before letting go the other. The toboggan, tethered behind him, bounded in the wild gusts. It tugged at his shoulders and banged against his legs, but he paid it no attention. The clinging snow was white on his back when he reached the summit.

"That was a thrill. Thanks, father-in-law, for changing me to the fast course. I haven't had such fun since the badger bit me. Are you going to try it too?"

"Oh, you think I'm afraid to? You think that spruce won't stop anybody but you? Well he and I have combined our magic many times. Together we've taken care of a lot of people. And every one of them got just what was coming to him. That tree won't let me down."

He took the toboggan line from Pikwak, knelt on the thin birch planks, and pushed with one foot.

"Here I come, spruce on the edge. Catch me."

Again the squeak of the downhill rush. Fast. Faster.

The long branches sway down, ready. The sharp little branchlets at their tips quiver their finger nails in anticipation. Then, at the last moment, the tree leans back and raises its arms.

The doctor blasts over the edge, soars on the toboggan like a gull, arcs down out of sight. Silence, silence, silence, a faraway splash, and then the sprinkle and tinkle of ice shards falling on the lightly frozen surface.

And that was the last that anybody ever heard or saw of Middlehawk. Pikwak and his wives lived happily forever after. Or anyway, for many years. Except once in a while when the children got mean and fought a little. Or when their mothers had a sisterly argument. Or when the husband forgot and called one of them auntie. But none of those things happened often.

Lost Arrows

He stood looking out over the rapid. The boulders were glistening black, with jagged edges. The water rushed white and loud between them.

"I am Nanabush," he shouted. "I am hungry. I want meat, but all the fat animals are on the other side. So quiet down, old river, while I cross you on your rocks."

A white wave curled up as high as his head. Splat! A smear of muddy foam shot off from it and slapped against his face. The rapid roared louder than ever.

He spat out some mud and wiped his face with his leather sleeve.

"All right. I understand that kind of sign-language. Now I will show you."

He hung his bow and his quiver of arrows over his shoulder and tied a thong around his waist to hold them in place. He ran out over the river rocks, jumping far, when he had to, from one to the next.

When he was half way across he called out, "See? You can't stop Nanabush, old river."

The next stone was wet, slanting, and slippery. His moccasin skidded. He fell into the water and was swept downstream. The current banged him against a rock and broke a chunk out of it. Then it slammed him against another. And others.

He kept on swimming. The river pulled him down and rolled him along the bottom boulders. He stroked and kicked his way up to the surface. Each time the water came choking

into his nose and mouth he blew it out again. And he didn't turn back.

At last he was carried into a quiet pool and felt gravel under his hands and knees. He crawled out on the bank. His clothes were torn. He had lost one of his moccasins. He was bruised all over. He was dripping as much blood as water.

He turned around and shouted, "See now, for yourself. You couldn't stop Nanabush."

The white water of the rapid bawled back at him.

"Who cares about Nanabush? I just wanted those straight, sharp arrows."

Nanabush grabbed for his quiver. All the arrows had been washed out of it.

"Keep them, then," he yelled. "I can make more."

But the trees here were weak and crooked and he had no stone arrowheads. He made three arrows anyway, whittled the ends into wooden points and feathered them with some gull feathers that he found beside the river.

He went up into the hills, walking quietly. His eyes were searching the woods ahead, and he stopped often to sniff the air and to listen.

When he got to the top of the second ridge he smelled bear, a musky whiff drifting up out of a ravine.

He climbed out on a projecting rock where he could look into the valley below. Sure enough, he saw a bear down there, scraping at a stump with his long curved claws.

"Kind greetings to you, black and hairy uncle," he shouted. "I am hungry. So come out from behind that snag where I can shoot you."

The bear looked up at him and at his arrows.

"Not with those stupid sticks," he growled. "I'm hungry too, and these worms are white and tender. So go away, nephew, and find a stumpful for yourself." He turned, broke off a piece of wood, and gobbled the grubs.

Nanabush could see only the black rump, where it stuck out from behind the stump. He took careful aim and let fly.

The bowstring sang. The arrow whispered. The wooden point went in just far enough to stick tight.

The bear gave a roar, swung around, and bit at the arrow. Then he stood up to make sure where it had come from.

Nanabush stepped closer, drew the bow into a deep curve, and shot again. But this arrow was crooked. It turned in its flight and missed.

By now, the bear was coming up the slope fast.

The third arrow splintered against the black uncle's shoulder. That didn't accomplish anything except to make him more angry.

Nanabush dropped the bow and ran.

The bear galloped after him, bounding and bouncing, as swift as a deer, only heavier and louder.

Nanabush was a good runner too. He dashed up and down the hills, crashed through the timber and splashed through the swamps. But soon he could hear the bear grunting and whuffing and clicking teeth.

His legs tried to run faster but his lungs were out of breath. He tripped over a log and fell flat into a soft bed of moss.

As he scrambled up, his hand sank deep into the moss and touched something hard. It was an antler that had been shed by a moose. Nanabush grabbed it, swung it up and held it to his head. He got to his feet and turned around, bellowing like a bull moose and pawing the ground.

The bear slid to a stop. He stood up, drooped his forepaws over his belly and spoke politely.

"I'm sorry to disturb you, brother moose. Did you happen to see a long-legged Indian with a hook nose in a hurry?"

"I'm not your brother," snorted Nanabush, "I don't keep track of your Indians nor notice their noses. Now get off my territory. And get fast, before I lose my sweet and gentle temper."

The bear dropped to all fours and went quickly away. Nanabush found a rotten stump and broke it open with the antler. The grubs tasted sweeter than he had expected.

Winter Games

Wolf slipped through the shoreline brush and strolled to where Turtle was jigging his line up and down through a hole in the ice. Suddenly it tightened and zigzagged back and forth in the water. Turtle wrapped it around his flipper and hauled up hard. But the fish was strong.

Wolf sat watching for a while before he spoke.

"I'd say that this tug-of-war is a tie. You can't drag him out of the water and he can't drag you in."

"Lend a hand, then, brother," said Turtle in his scratchy voice.

Wolf picked up the loose end of the line and pulled. A big, toothy head slid out of the hole, and then the long, spotted, flopping body.

"Thank you, friend jackfish," said Turtle. "Now you won't have to swim in the cold water any more. So stop bouncing and rest comfortably with your friends who came up before you."

"That's a nice pile of fish," said Wolf. "Me, I haven't been doing that well. But I did catch up with a deer last week, and I still have a quarter hanging back in the woods. Venison is nice, but I love fish."

Turtle had baited up again and was watching his line fade into the deep dark.

"I never was much of a deer hunter," he said. "Would you trade meat for fish?"

Wolf stretched himself long and low while he thought about this offer. Then he shortened again and came up with a different proposal.

"What do you say we make it a little exciting. Let's race, winner take all?"

Turtle's wife poked her head up out the hole. She said something to her man in tortoise, then slid back under the water.

"I can't understand that dialect. What's the word?"

"She says I should take you up on your sporting proposition. But my legs are shorter than yours, so she suggests that we should each do it his own way. You run and I'll swim. See that dark spot on the ice out there?"

Wolf squinted.

"I see it. Looks like another fishing place."

"That's right. We've got this line of six holes strung along the shore in a circle back to here. I'll poke my head up from each of them as I come to it, so that we can each see how we're doing. But first, you get the meat so that the prize will be ready for whoever's the swifter."

"Fair enough," said Wolf and he loped off into the bush. He came back with the quarter slung over his shoulder and laid it beside the fish.

Turtle's wife drew a starting line for Wolf where the wind had blown most of the snow away.

"Take your marks," she said, tense as a turtle ever gets, but speaking clearly now in a loud, official voice.

Turtle leaned forward over the hole, with his knees bent and his toes hooked over the edge. Wolf crouched behind his line.

"Ready.

"Get set.

"Go!"

Turtle made a racing dive. Wolf's toenails skidded on the ice so that he got off to a slow start. Once under way, though, he ran as though an over-weight caribou were just one jump ahead of him.

As he neared the first hole, he saw a dark object rise over its edge. Coming closer he could make out the triangular turtle head. It winked at him and disappeared.

Wolf was amazed. "I'm going to have to run faster."

But at hole two the turtle came up some distance ahead of him, looked back, smiled, and dived again. Wolf was running as he had never run before.

The turtle crawled out of the third hole way in the lead. He stood on the ice while Wolf came panting up, then waved an encouraging gesture and splashed down. Wolf was running so fast that he was hardly touching the ice, soaring like a low-flying owl.

The fourth hole was half way around the lake. This time the turtle croaked at him. "Come on, slowpoke, you can do better than that!"

Wolf swirled toward the fifth hole like a gust of snow in a blizzard, but he didn't get any closer to the turtle that time either. The poor predator was gasping now and his eyes were beginning to bug out.

He couldn't hold that pace any longer and came lurching and blowing up to the sixth hole like a moose trying to run in deep snow. And yet, there was the turtle, only just ahead of him now. He spent some of his little remaining wind in a feeble but happy holler.

"Ho, there, moss-back brother! I can see that you're weakening. Now I'm going to pass you by!"

The turtle dived without answering.

Wolf blasted off in one last flare of energy, but that faded fast. When he staggered toward the starting hole his tail was dragging on the snow. Turtle crawled out well ahead of him, fresh and sprightly as a fawn. His woman, chanting, stamped her scaly feet in a little dance of triumph. They tried to get the venison over to the water but it was too heavy for them.

"Well, I never would have thought that you had that much speed in you," gasped Wolf. "I'll help you, but let me get my breath first."

While they waited, Turtle passed fish to his woman and she swam away with them. Wolf figured that she must be taking them to some cache under the ice.

When he felt better he carried the quarter to the hole. The wife towed it away and came back quickly. Turtle was waiting for her at the edge with a big round walleye pike. She grabbed it out of his flippers and swirled under. Wolf sat down with his tongue hanging out. Still breathing hard, he stared sadly across the lake.

What was that, over there at the first hole? A turtle? It must be the woman. No, she had just popped up beside him to snatch a bluegill from her husband. He looked again, farther away. Suddenly he stiffened. Another turtle was coming out of another hole. And another.

Turtle, watching him, grabbed a yellow perch and dashed for the water.

Wolf pounced. His teeth slithered off the hard shell, knocking Turtle off his feet. He dropped the fish.

Wolf skidded past him, then whirled around. Turtle sprinted for the hole. Wolf's jaws snapped shut, but all he got was a splash of ice water in his face.

He stood there for a moment, his whiskers dripping, watching that rounded reptile swim way down into the darkness. Then he took a few steps back toward the shore.

Now just one minute. They hadn't got all the fish!

He turned again. The turtle-wife had made off with the perch. Now she was trying to get the last fish, but it was frozen to the ice. Wolf came charging back. She took one more unsuccessful jerk, then plopped into the water.

The abandoned sunfish stared at Wolf and the world with indifferent eyes. He nosed it, wondering why she had tried so hard to get this flat little bundle of bones. He tore it loose and munched it thoughtfully as he walked toward the woods.

The Hunters

Nanabush would be all right now. He was tired and hungry. The wind from the east shook the branches above him and turned his sweat cold. Fast-flying snow whipped around him, biting in through even the smallest openings in his clothing. But the deer had been kind to him. He would be all right now.

He dragged his kill into the shelter of a thicket. There, with cold-stiff fingers, he skinned and cut it. The meat would quickly freeze, and he would have food for a long time.

He made a roof of poles, thatched it with spruce branches, and built a little fire in front of it. He sharpened a forked stick, stuck a slice of meat on it, and held it close to the flame.

The wind shook the roof above him, swaying the boughs wildly. The frame squeaked and groaned.

"Ho there," Nanabush called. "Ho, damp and chilly uncle. I know all your tricks, because the west wind is my father. My lean-to is bound to a pine tree at one end and braced with stout poles at the other. You can't tear it away. Besides, I'm wrapped in a fresh deerskin, fur side in."

The wind whipped around the corner and blew smoke around his head. He coughed and wiped his eyes.

"That whiff of smoke smelled good. It goes with the smell of venison dripping juice on the embers. So blow hard, Uncle East. Blow and have your fun."

The wind groaned and swirled a handful of snow into his face. He smiled and brushed it off.

"Thanks again, uncle. By this hot fire, that cool little sprinkle was just right."

He had taken the cooking stick and was raising the meat for the first bite when the jealous wind tried another trick. It grabbed the tops of two tall birch trees and rubbed them together, making a terrible wail. Nanabush paused, the steak poised in front of his open mouth, a pained expression on his face.

Scre-e-ech.

"Be quiet, uncle," he shouted. "Now I am ready to take my first bite of this nice piece of venison, and I don't like that sour song."

Scre-e-e-ech.

"I'm not going to have my dinner spoiled by your unmerciful music!" He laid aside the skin and pushed the end of the stick into the thawed earth near the fire so that the meat would keep warm. Then he shinnied up one of the birches to the place where the trees were rubbing. He took hold of each of them and began to weave them together.

When the wind saw what he was up to it blew the trees so hard that that one of them came bending down on Nanabush's arm and clamped it in a fork of the other. And there he was, caught like a fox in a trap.

He jerked and pushed, but could not shake free. His feet searched the treetrunk and found a branch to stand on. He hung and clung there, shivering.

He heard a long howl. It came again, closer. Then he saw dark forms running between the trees. Running fast and smoothly. They seemed to float over the boulders and fallen timber.

"Brothers and sisters," he shouted. "There is nothing here."

The wolves stopped. The old leader lifted her muzzle and called back.

"Who are you, and what do you want of us?"

"I am Nanabush. I am stuck up here in the birch branches. I just wanted to let you know that there is nothing that would interest you in the bush below me. No meat or anything like that. So keep on your way, and I wish you good hunting."

"Come on, children," said the old one. "We'd better look into this."

She turned and pushed into the thicket, the others close behind her. They found the pile of cut-up meat and ate it.

"All right, nephew," said the wind, "you can go now. I just wanted to teach you to appreciate good music. I like to help with my young relatives' education whenever I can."

He stopped blowing. The birches sprang back, freeing
Nanabush. He slid stiffly down the trunk, started to walk toward where he had left the meat. The wolves circled around
him, watching him, their pointed ears standing up on end.

The old leader was holding down a piece of the carcass
with her paw while she tore at the ribs. She looked up at him
and yawned. A wide, comfortable yawn.

"What big teeth you have, grandmother. You and your family ate my deer. You wouldn't eat me too, would you?" He took
a step back toward the tree.

"Relax," she answered. "Humans are not our dish. Moose, yes, mice, yes, marmots, yes, men, no."

"What's the matter with men?" asked Nanabush, crossly. "Aren't we just as good as the other animals?"

"I'm sorry," said the grandmother, "but my name is Alfa and I always tell the truth, even when it's rude. Men just don't smell good."

Nanabush walked over and spread his hands to the fire.

"If you can't stand me you can move upwind. It's cold in those high branches."

He heard a crack as strong jaws broke open a bone to get at the marrow.

"We Indians share our food with the poor and hungry."

"It's the same with us," said Alfa. "When we have meat, nobody goes without. I saved your share for you." She picked up the stick, still speared through the cooked steak, and carried it to him.

"Thanks, grandmother. This will do me for supper. But the rest of the meat is gone and I will need more tomorrow."

"So will we," said the old wolf. "We won't worry about that tonight, though."

When everybody had finished eating, gnawing, and crunching they lay down and went to sleep, Nanabush in his brush shelter, the wolves curled up in the snow, with their tails covering their noses.

Nanabush woke in pale winter sunlight. Wolves were moving around him, frisking, stretching their legs and their jaws, arching their backs. Some of the younger ones were sparring with each other, pushing, snarling and snapping rather earnestly but not doing any damage.

"What's for breakfast?" asked Nanabush.

"That depends," said Alfa. "Breakfast has to be caught. And it might be tomorrow's breakfast or next week's. Right now we're warming up for the hunt. Would you care to join us?"

"I guess I'd better." He began to bend, stretch, and jog around. He strung his bow and loosed an imaginary arrow. When some of the wolves began to howl the hunting song, he sang along with them. There were answers from the forest and several came hurrying in. The leader called over a long-legged young male. His black coat was tinged with blue.

"Tooth, you stay with Nanabush. He is a wise man with great power, but he will need a guide. See that he doesn't get lost, hurt himself, freeze his feet, or fall head-first into a snowdrift. And keep him moving. Don't let him get too far behind."

"Oh Granny," Tooth yipped. "I'm a hunter, not a baby-sitter. I want to run with the pack."

But she was already gone. The others loped after her at an easy jogging gait.

Easy for the wolves, but hard going for the man, even in the shallow snow of early winter. Tooth was barking at him to hurry, but he couldn't hold the pace.

At noon, though, they came out on the crest of a low hill and found many of the wolves lying in the snow, sleeping. Alfa and a few others stood looking out over the broad valley below. Nanabush could see black spots that circled and glided above a far away place.

"Deer are there," said the grandmother. "The ravens are telling us. Stumpjumper and Graywoman, go down and look the situation over."

Nanabush scraped away a space until he reached the dead leaves beneath, then flopped down gratefully. He liked this wolf idea of resting any time you get the chance.

When he woke, he and Tooth were alone again. But this time they did not have far to go. As they crossed another low rise they saw caribou ahead. They were nipping on the brush and pawing snow away to get at brown grass and ground foliage.

The wolves were sauntering around them, inspecting each one thoughtfully, making no effort at concealment. Neither the hunters nor their prey seemed excited by the presence of the other.

Suddenly a wolf rushed at a browsing doe. She glanced at him, grabbed one more bite of willow, tossed her head, and sped away in a cloud of flying snow. He took a few galloping bounds after her, then seemed to lose interest and resumed his stroll. The doe stopped. For a few moments she stood, munching her mouthful of twigs, and watching her easily-discouraged pursuer. Nanabush thought that he saw her shrug her shoulders. Then she turned away and went on with her feeding.

"Why aren't the stupid things scared?" he asked. "Don't they know what we're here for? And what's the matter with the hunters? Are they lazy or something? I'm hungry."

"You're always hungry," said Tooth. "But everything is in order. We and the deer have been doing business together for a long time and each knows what to expect of the other. If it weren't for them we'd starve. And they'd be a sad and sickly lot if they didn't have us to watch over them."

"Watch over them is right," said Nanabush. "That seems to be all anybody does is watch. I should think that the wolves would at least try to run a deer down."

"No way can we catch any that are in good running order. We get some fawns in the spring and summer, but now they're faster than the grown-ups. The scouts are checking the herd for a possible candidate—a sick one or a senior citizen that's getting a little stiff in the joints. That's one good thing about being a caribou—you never get really decrepit. When winter comes we take care of the old ones."

"It just doesn't seem right," said Nanabush, "for us wolves to be strolling around as though we'd all lost our appetites while the caribou go on chewing brush."

"We and they will need all the strength and fat we have before the winter's over," said Tooth. "No use in either party tearing around and burning up a lot of energy until a real chase begins."

The leisurely hunt continued. Other caribou came in to join the herd. Each one was observed and several were tested.

As dusk closed in, one of them flunked the test. The examiner's expert eye caught the weakness in her stride. He yipped a little and ran after her, keeping to the trail that she had broken. The pack followed.

She gave them a good run. It was night when Nanabush and Tooth caught up with them. The wolves were sprawled in a circle of tramped-down snow. Much of the carcass had been eaten but there was still some left for latecomers. Nanabush bit and tore at his piece as fiercely as any wolf. And when one of them got too near him, he growled.

The second day began like the first. The herd had moved on, but the wolves soon caught up with them. Nanabush and Tooth followed. There were the tracks of many short chases but no packed circle, no blood in the snow. They came up with some of the wolves resting along the trail.

Nanabush took his bow and two arrows in his left hand. The arrows had stone heads, with the edges chipped away to slicing sharpness. He began to move ahead.

"Hold on there," whispered Tooth. "You'll spook them."

"I know how to hunt deer," said Nanabush. "And I don't do it sitting in the snow."

He walked off to one side until he was directly downwind of the feeding herd. Then he moved silently toward them, keeping low and behind cover. The snow was soft and he stepped carefully. But suddenly he heard a wild snort ahead, and the clicking of hooves.

A scout came trotting back to report.

"Those deer are really travelling. We didn't notice any slowpokes."

"They get around," said Alfa, "and they know about men. They'll go a long way now. We'd better find us some other deer."

She turned to Nanabush. "If you'd been alone you might have scored. They keep sentinels on watch when they know we're near. When we come on a single deer we'll let you stalk it. But in this herd work, you'd better let us do the hunting."

They found no more signs of game that day or the next. From time to time they slept a while and then went on. In spite of Tooth's urgings, Nanabush fell far behind. On the third day without food he was weak with hunger and said so.

When a rabbit streaked across the trail, Tooth took after it and brought it back to him. That helped, but by evening they were alone in a silent forest. Nanabush could go no farther. Glumly, they made their simple camp.

Nanabush was wakened by a cold nose poked under his chin. The leader and Tooth were standing beside him.

"It's not going to work out," she said. "I came back this time, but we can't delay the hunt any longer. I will go to the others now and get on with the work. Tooth, you stay with Nanabush. Show him how to make meat. If you can't teach him, be sure, at least, that he doesn't starve."

"Whenever you do somebody a favor," said Tooth, "that's when you get stuck for more charity. This guy is hopeless. If he doesn't get something to eat every couple of days he bellyaches about being hungry. But he couldn't run down the feeblest old invalid that ever stumbled behind a herd.

"And you saw how he doesn't even defend his own territory. He calls trespassers to his kill instead of chasing them off."

"All those are reasons why you will have to stay with him," said the grandmother. "We can't hold back the hunting pack for him. And it wouldn't be right to just leave him alone in the winter woods. You can see that.

"We hadn't planned to hunt the Waywasibi for another year. The moose in that valley needed a rest. But you two won't bother them much. You can go over there. Just be sure not to kill more than you need.

"Look after Nanabush through the deep snow months. You can join us when the ice goes out. Goodby until then." She faded silently into the forest.

"As you see, I'm stuck with you," Tooth snarled. "But that's only till the river breaks up. From then on, my friend, you'll be on your own. You're not my choice of a hunting partner."

"Well, Tooth," said Nanabush, "I don't know that I care all that much for your company either. Still, I do need to eat. So let's give it a try and see how it goes."

They crossed a range of low hills and came down at evening to the Waywasibi. The river at this point was a lazy stream that wound its unhurried way under the ice across an expanse of swampland. Islands of spruce and cedar stood dark in the white muskeg.

Four years earlier, in a particularly hungry winter, the moose population here had been hunted down to a low level. Since then the wolves had stayed away, letting the area lie fallow.

Almost at once, Tooth's nose went down into a depression in the snow. He blew out his breath and inhaled deeply. Then he lifted his head and smiled at Nanabush.

"This smells good. An old bull. He maybe needs our help."

He started along the track, then turned back.

"I told you about caribou, and now, before we go any farther, I'd better fill you in on moose. These are a different kind of deer. Don't count on them to take off any time you make a pass at them. And their big, sharp hooves are bad medicine."

"When you run at a moose and he stands and stares at you, take it easy. Don't think that you can just tear in, and pull him over. A lot of young wolves get broken bones that way and some have their heads split.

"The trick is to nip and feint at him, try to get him running. If he charges, put your tail between your legs and get out of the way. If he holds his ground, forget him. Same thing if he runs off fast and clean. But if you hear him wheeze a little, or see that he's stiff or confused or limping, that's the time to turn on the heat.

"Don't get too close to this first one. Stand back and watch me work him. That way you'll see how it's done and maybe you can help with others. But be careful. I wouldn't want to have to tell the old lady that something happened to you. You're really too slow for this kind of hunting."

"I may be slow," said Nanabush, "but I have some feathered friends here who can fly fast." He took out two arrows and held them along with the bow in his left hand, ready for quick shots.

"So get on with it, Tooth. Less education, please, and more action."

"All right, big red hunter. Since you want so much action, let's go."

He scudded away like a low-flying cloud, tail floating out behind, feet seeming to just brush the snowy hummocks. Then he was out of sight.

Nanabush followed. He met the wolf sauntering back.

71

"Nothing wrong with that old guy. He took off like a three-year-old and ran into a spruce island. But that's all right, we'll find a better prospect soon."

"Let's not give him up that easily. I haven't eaten anything for three days unless you count that one skinny little rabbit. So show me where your elderly friend is hiding out and we'll see what we can do about him."

"There's just the two of us," said Tooth. "And even if we had the pack I don't think that we could accomplish much with this one. But there's no use trying to talk sense into you. I'll take you to him and you can see for yourself."

When they came in sight of the island, Nanabush climbed up on an old cedar stump for a better view. The spruce thicket pushed out several points into the open muskeg. One of these almost touched a similar arm extended by another island.

Nanabush slid down from the stump.

"Just wait here, Tooth, until I get out on that narrows. But don't go to sleep either. We haven't got much daylight left.

"As soon as I get to the trees, go into the island from the opposite side and help the old boy find his way in my direction. He'll likely go for that nice sheltered passageway of his own accord, but you make sure that he doesn't get any other ideas."

"All right. I see what you've got in mind. I don't think that it's going to work, but I'll do my part. At least you'll learn something and you're not likely to get hurt. He won't be so handy with his hooves while he's running on them.

"But don't be a hero. Just slash him, and turn him if you can. Don't grab him by the nose. I'll be right behind him and we'll see what we can do."

"Don't worry, Tooth. I won't grab him by the nose."

With Tooth's guidance, the bull found the planned path, and went down under the impact of two close-range arrows. Nanabush thanked and bled him. Then, while the wolf tore at a haunch, he dressed the rest of the carcass. Even in the gathering darkness his knife found its way quickly to the weak spots in the heavy joints.

A wind came down the valley from the north, sharpening the evening chill and dusting the hunters with fresh snow. They took shelter under a projecting rock ledge, screened by dense spruce. Nanabush made fire and cooked his dinner. Tooth curled up in the shallow little cave.

"This isn't so bad," he said. "And I like those birds of yours that sing when they fly. But we've got lots of meat now. I don't suppose we should hunt again for a while."

"We'd better get one or two more moose while they're around," said Nanabush. "It's cold. Today's kill will keep."

"It won't rot, but it won't keep either. If we don't stay close to it until it's finished, the little foxes will spoil it, and probably a wolverine."

But they took that chance. In the morning they were out again, anxious to experiment further with this combination of wolf nose, wolf speed and man's arrows.

Tooth soon located a cow with a yearling calf. He circled them, hustling them downwind toward his partner's stand.

The mother kept just behind the calf, following him, covering his rear. The youngster was awkward but big for his age, and stubborn.

As they approached the ambush he lurched to one side. Tooth darted in at him. Keeping a wary eye on the mother, he came too close to the son. A youthful but heavy hoof shot out, caught him in the shoulder, tumbled him into the snow.

Instantly the cow charged. Tooth scrambled to his feet and ran.

"This way!" Nanabush called.

Tooth swerved toward him, but he was limping badly. The moose was close behind him. Her mane was erect, her neck stetched out, head low, ears laid back, tongue sticking out ahead. She was gaining on the wolf at every step.

Behind her came the yearling. This was fun. Maybe he could get in another kick.

As the flying procession swept toward Nanabush, he took careful aim. The arrow curved to the target he had chosen— the bouncing flesh of the calf's shoulder-hump. He slid to a stop, with a wail as desperate as though he had been mortally wounded.

The cow whirled back, nosed him, hurried him away from the danger. Nanabush ran toward the stumbling Tooth. He had another arrow notched, but the two moose went plowing off through the snow.

The wolf crouched while Nanabush bent over him. His fingers prodded, searching beneath the wincing fur.

"Cheer up, Tooth. You won't walk the spirit road tonight, But what was that advice you were giving me? Something about keeping away from hooves? We'd better find a younger baby for you next time."

Tooth was content to rest for the next three days. Nanabush carried in wood and kept them both comfortable with fire. He went back to the passage between the spruce islands. The foxes had not failed to find the meat, but a fair amount of it remained. He hung the tattered pieces in one of the trees in front of the cave.

They went over the details of their successful hunt and of the more recent failure, studying moose tactics for the future. They scratched drawings in the dust designing safe and effective strategies. And they agreed that from this time on they would be brothers.

Tooth's shoulder mended fast. Soon they were out on the muskeg again, using the flights and charges of the moose, turning both to their own advantage. The wolf would lure or drive the big deer to the arrows, or dodge and nip and tease around one of them, turning his rushes, holding him until Nanabush arrived.

That was a good winter for hunting. Too good.

In the strengthening sun of the month when snowshoes break through, they were sitting beside a fresh kill.

"If I put on any more weight I won't be able to run," said Tooth. "We'd better lay off the moose for a while."

Nanabush belched comfortably. "Get the meat while the meat is there. As you once told me, we may need all the fat and energy we can gather before the winter is over."

"I'd say that the winter is already over. The upstream rapids are open and the river ice is turning black. It may break up tomorrow. And grandma will be coming back."

He looked at the half-eaten moose. "We didn't even clean up the shanks, let alone crunch bones."

Nanabush sat up quickly.

"Get away, you!"

He snatched up a stick and threw it with power and accuracy. The fox yelped and darted away from the carcass. Then it paused, stood watching for a moment, and came sneaking back.

"Look at him," said Tooth. "He's so fat he can't dodge. But still he won't wait for us to leave. It's getting so that even the ravens will eat nothing but steaks and chops. Alfa's going to see the leftovers. And she's not going to like it."

"The evil spirits don't like it either," said Nanabush. "Some manedog have been showing up at night, lately. I wasn't going to tell you about them. It's not good to blab about dreams. But these concern you and I think you should know."

"Well cough it up, then." Tooth was alert. "Which manedog?"

"The worst ones. Especially the missikenabekog. Last night one of those big snakes came to me. I could see him clearly, swaying there under the trees in the moonlight with his horns brushing the branches. And he was talking to me."

"Was he complaining about our hunting?"

"I gathered that it's got past the point of complaining. They're going to do something about it."

"You should have as much power as they do. That is, if all your bragging is true. As you keep telling me, you're about half god yourself. Your father was the west wind."

"Ah, but there was my mother. A woman is only a woman. In any case they can get at me through you."

"Don't worry about me. The missikenabekog hate humans more than animals. They steal puppies, but they wouldn't waste their time and their wickedness on a grown wolf. Really, I'm a lot more scared of grandma. She gets mean when she catches somebody overkilling."

Nanabush leaned forward, elbows on knees, and rested his head in his hands. "Keep quiet. I'm trying to get back to that dream."

After a while he reached out and ran a hand through the dark fur on Tooth's back.

"Now listen to me, brother. I can't remember it all, and I wouldn't tell you if I could. No use bringing any more misfortune on you than the manedog have in mind.

But I'll let you in on one thing that you need to know. Stay away from running water. Even the smallest trickle. That's where the missikenabekog hang out. They even follow the veins of water under the earth."

Tooth yawned and arched his back under the stroking hand. "Sure, brother, whatever you say. Got any other charms or secret instructions, like something to protect me from grandma?"

"If you're that scared of her, I suppose we'd better stop hunting. We'll clean up some of the meat that we've left lying around the woods."

The south wind came that night. They woke to the splash of water trickling from the rock ledge overhead. The spicy

75

pungency of aspen buds was in the air. And when the sun beat down into the bush they caught another smell, the carrion odor of rotting moose.

They slept most of that day, waking at times to play at fighting. Tooth pounced, snapped, leaped away. Nanabush struck hard at him, knowing that the wolf would be gone when the blow arrived. At evening they went to the latest carcass and picked at it.

As they walked back to the cave, Tooth came to a sudden stop, rigid, his tail erect. "See, brother! Over there in the alders."

Nanabush looked in the direction of the pointed muzzle. After a while he made out the form of a whitetail doe standing motionless in the tangle of dark red trunks.

"Easy, now. She's exactly what we don't need. Come on." He walked toward the camp. The wolf whined a little and then followed, stopping several times to look back.

In the morning they saw the doe again. And again Tooth froze.

"She'd make a lovely change from spoiled moose," he whimpered.

"Just get her out of your mind, brother. She may have been sent by the manedog."

So it was another day of rough play, eating old meat, and dozing in the sun. Nanabush was wakened by the chill of lengthening spruce shadows. He was alone.

He called, got no answer, walked up to the knob above the cave and called some more. Then he found a tall, hollow stump and swung a pole against it, booming loud enough to guide a lost brother home from far away. He went on pounding for a long time. Echos came rolling back from the bluffs above the river but there was no other response.

At first light he was out and searching the forest floor. He soon picked up the doe's hoof prints, driven deep into the leaves and soft earth. She had been running hard. And yes, here were the familiar pug-marks in pursuit. They lead him up out of the Waywasibi valley, over a ridge of hills, and down into a dark ravine.

The creek along its bottom was free of ice and swelled with meltwater, but the doe had crossed it at a bound. The wolf spoor ended there. Just ended. No blood, no signs of a struggle. Tooth might have taken wing and flown away.

Nanabush hurried down the stream, searching among the rocks and dead timber along its banks, finding no clues. The creek widened, came out from the shadow of the trees, curved around a sandbar, and entered a lake. A twisted old cedar reached out toward the mouth, and a blue-gray bird with a long bill was sitting on one of its branches.

Nanabush stepped out on the sand beneath him. "Ho, you up there. Are you watching the sunrise?"

"No, I'm waiting for my breakfast. The missikenabekog have somebody down under the water. I'm watching for the guts to float up."

"Would the victim, by any chance, be that young, blue wolf known as Tooth?"

The bird gave him a sharp look. "You must be Nanabush. I'm not saying anything more. I wouldn't want to get in wrong with the manedog."

He hopped to a higher branch.

But not high enough. Nanabush jumped and grabbed at him, got him by the headfeathers.

"Now little friend, tell me all about it," he said, giving a pretty good pull.

"I'll tell you everything, Nanabush. Only don't jerk my hair any more. If my head comes off it won't be able to tell you much."

"Then sing your song, keep it sweet and true, and don't forget anything."

He eased the pressure just a little. The bird shuddered and then spoke.

"Whenever the weather is sunny the evil ones come out at exactly noon to talk and sleep on this beach. I was sitting here when they held their last council.

"You maybe know Missepishu. He's that pale gray water lynx as big as a bear, very old and very wise. Anyway, he spoke first.

" 'We've got to do something about Nanabush and his pet wolf, Tooth. They're killing too many moose. If we let them continue like that there will be none left.' "

The bird looked sideways at Nanabush.

"The bad gods do have some good ideas."

"Never mind the theology. Just go on with your story."

"The great brown bear with the black face, holiest and meanest of the manedog, spoke next. He called you the bastard of the west wind and said that you were getting too big for your breechclout.

"A frog monster was spread out in the shallow water. 'I hear everything that's said,' he croaked. 'Now the talk is that Nanabush is more powerful than us sacred ghouls. And that he may soon move against us.'

" 'That's just gossip,' said the biggest missikenabek. 'He wouldn't dare.'

"Old lynx Missepishu frowned,

" 'Don't be too sure of that. He's a sly one. And he looks out for the Indians. I don't think he approves of your taste for babies. He might call in your enemies, the thunderers.'

"The bear stood up, his paws drooped over his belly, and growled. 'If he has all that power, I say that we'd better hit first.'

"Everybody looked at Missepishu. He was just sitting there not moving except that his black ear tufts twitched a little.

"'It would have to be done quietly, so that no thunderer that happened to be passing over would see it.'

" 'Then just leave it to us snakes. We'll go up the creeks and lay for those two poachers under cover of the trees. We'll drown Tooth for sure, and maybe the wind-Indian too.'

" 'If you kill only the wolf,' said the old manedo, 'Nanabush may find out what happened and come against us for revenge.'

" 'All the better if he does. Our hides are weapon-proof. His arrows will bounce off us. If he tries to get tough we'll kill him too.'

"The Lynx spoke in a little cat voice, not much more than a whisper. 'What if he knows about our soft shadows?'

" 'He's gotten to be more man than manedo,' said the serpent. 'He won't remember that dreams and shadows are real, and that what men call real is nothing but dreams and shadows.'

"That seemed to put everybody at ease. They all flopped down on the warm sand and went to sleep. And I flew away.

"But last night I was back on my roost over the river mouth. I heard a loud rippling and here came a pair of horns cutting through the water. When they passed under me I could see the big snake towing what was left of some animal with dark fur. And that's all I know."

"Thank you, little friend," said Nanabush. "You've told me enough. I'm afraid I've mussed your hair so badly that your wife will never be able to comb it smooth. . . . So I give you this to make you handsome anyway." Quickly he took from his neck a white bone necklace and dropped it over the bird's head. "Wear this always. From this time on your name will be Kingfisher. And now I must hurry. It's almost noon."

He ran out on the point, scraped a groove in the sand, laid his bow and stone-tipped arrows in it, and covered them. Then he stood up and turned himself into an old pine stump.

He was just in time. His shadow was pointing straight north.

Right away the water swirled and the manedog came splashing, crawling, and wriggling out of it.

"That was a good dinner," said Missepishu. "I never really cared much for wolf older than six weeks, but that one hit the spot."

"Thank you," said the biggest missikenabek. "He was nicely fattened, wasn't he? If I do say so myself. And here is the pelt."

He held up a blue-black fur. Missepishu pawed it lovingly.

"I was surprised how easy it was to catch him," said the snake. "That little doe knew her business. But I thought that Nanabush would take better care of his follower."

"Now we'll lie down in the sun and sleep him off." He turned to the lynx. "The skin is a gift for you."

The old manedo spread the fur on the sand and curled up on it. His eyes closed, but opened again, big and yellow with narrow black slits.

"We'd best be careful, though. By now Nanabush knows that something has happened to his doggy brother. He may even blame us for it. That's the way he is."

He raised up on his haunches and looked around. "It seems to me that something's not quite right about this landscape. . . . That pine stump. It looks as though it had been standing there for a many years, but I don't remember it."

"I'll check it out," said the snake. He slithered over the sand, wrapped himself around the pine, and gave a terrible squeeze. It hurt Nanabush so that he was afraid that they would hear a gasp. But what came out of him was just the groaning and squeaking of weathered wood.

"It's nothing but an old stump," said the missikenabek as he unwound.

"I suppose you're right," said the lynx. "But we can't be too careful when we're dealing with Nanabush. Brother Mukwa, give the stump a tickle and see if you can make it laugh."

The bear came lumbering up from the water, lifted his paw, and raked the old pine from its branch to its roots. There was no sound but the splintering.

"That's good enough for me," he said, and laid down in the sand. The others did the same, and soon all were snoring like faraway thunder.

Nanabush changed back into himself. His ribs ached and the claw-marks were bleeding. But he dug up his weapons, tip-toed over to the lynx, and drove an arrow deep into his shadow in the sand.

Missepishu sprang up, his eyes wide, gave a terrible screech, started for his enemy and fell, claws reaching out for him, but not quite touching.

Nanabush stepped clear of the curving knives, snatched up the wolfskin, swung it over his shoulder, and tucked the ends under his belt.

He turned just in time to see the main missikenabek come swirling across the beach at him. Startled, he aimed an arrow at the head. The stone tip struck with a clang and the shaft fell broken on the sand. The next arrow stabbed into the approaching shadow. The snake collapsed in a blur of lashing coils.

Nanabush turned and ran for the hills. He ran hard but stiffly, his body hurting from the serpent's grip and the bear's gash.

Close behind he heard the pounding of holy paws and the screaming, roaring, and hissing of many manedog.

"I raked him well," the bear-god shouted. "He won't go far." Indeed, Tooth's skin was already soaked and dripping a red trail on the leaves.

Nanabush burst out of the shoreline brush into a natural clearing, an expanse of stony grassland that rose above the river flats. A little fox manedo, faster than his heavier colleagues, was snapping at his heels. As they went up the slope this small demon got his teeth into a moccasin and jerked skillfully sideways. Nanabush went down like a hamstrung moose.

He fell across a mound of freshly-dug earth and his head rammed into some kind of a hole. As he lay there, gasping and half-stunned, he heard a low whistle. A squeaky voice spoke out of the hill.

"Down here, and quick."

The fox had him by the ankle now. Nanabush kicked him off, struggled forward into the darkness of a narrow tunnel.

"I'm widening the burrow ahead," said the voice. "You fill it in behind."

A stream of earth and stones came shooting against his face and shoulders.

"Hey, stop that," he called. "You're getting sand in my eyes."

The flow of dirt ceased and a grizzled face looked back. "Excuse me. What did you say?"

On the hillside behind them the bear was roaring. "Out of my way, you silly little varmints. Let me get at that hole!"

"Never mind," Nanabush said to the face. "Just keep the dirt coming."

He wormed forward, scraping the rubble back with his hands.

There was a thud and a squeal out there. Powerful claws ripped into the hillside. Daylight broke in from behind. Ahead, Nanabush saw the broad hindquarters of a female woodchuck. These were working again, pumping back swift surges of earth.

He pushed against her, drawing up his feet, as an enormous paw came searching into the tunnel. The claw-tips grazed a moccasin.

"I've got him," the bear shouted, straining to reach farther. "Almost, anyway. I will in another minute."

Suddenly Nanabush realized that space had opened ahead again. He squirmed into it. The bear stretched and scrabbled. The woodchuck's feet shoveled back dirt, moving swiftly into the hill. Nanabush followed, and pushed the earth into a barrier behind them.

They were in total darkness again. The shaft was turning uphill. The bear had gone back to digging but he had wasted crucial seconds trying to make the snatch while the woodchuck had been working.

There were shouts from the other manedog. "Deeper, Mukwa, deeper and faster and not so wide."

The sound of digging stopped for a moment as the bear turned, reared, and roared.

"Silence, runts! I've got to open a real hole. Not just for an Indian or a groundhog. For a superbear."

But the Indian and the groundhog were drawing away from him fast now. The cries of the manedog grew fainter. Then, as he piled more dirt behind him, Nanabush could hear nothing but the sound of digging ahead.

They came to a side passage that ran off at an angle from the main shaft. The woodchuck turned into it. "Pack a wall in tight and smooth and solid there," she called back. "Don't let it show. I doubt that they'll get this far, but if they do, we want them to keep straight on in. There's plenty of hill."

Later they reached a wider place, a chamber where Nanabush could raise himself on an elbow.

"Make yourself at home here," said the lady of the burrow. "Best stay until night. The gods will go back to the lake then and I'll dig you out." She ambled off down one of two other passages that left the den.

Nanabush rolled out the wolfskin and lay on it. His ribs and joints still pained him but the bleeding had stopped. The air was good and he thought he could see some light in one of the entrances. This must be close to the top of the hill.

At last that faint light disappeared. Soon he heard the woodchuck digging. He followed her and came out under the stars.

"You have done me a great kindness," he said. "So now I am going to do something for you and your descendants."

"You shall grow fat and comfortable without having to kill meat. You will eat leaves, grass, bark, and flowers. You may doze in the sun while others hunt."

"Well, thanks," replied the groundhog. "Not that it's such a big change in diet. But we're glad that Nanabush approves. And I'm sure you won't mind if we occasionally knock off a grasshopper or other sweet little squirmer. We're not consecrated vegetarians. . . . I'll leave you now. Dream well."

Next day, sitting upright on her earth mound, she saw Nanabush on the ridge above. He had made a fire and was cooking something. She could see that the wolfskin was spread on a flat stone beside him.

It seemed to her that he was talking, either to the skin or to some invisible person. Later she heard, faintly, the sound of singing and drumming. When the chant ended, Nanabush knelt, raised the skin, blew on it, and laid it back on the stone.

After a while, the fur began to move, to lift a little at its center. It rose higher, filling out, taking the shape of a live wolf. It stepped toward Nanabush. The woodchuck shook her head and waddled into her burrow.

"So, brother, you have brought me back," said Tooth. "An unusual favor, if it is a favor. To what do I owe this honor?"

"It is not a favor," said Nanabush. "But it is an honor. I have work for you. First, though, we will eat together. Our last supper."

He set a bark dish of meat and rice on the rock between them. Tooth ate slowly, so that each would have an equal share.

When they had finished, Nanabush spoke.

"You have walked on the spirit road. You know that it is rough, hard to follow, blocked by obstacles and menaced by dangers. Many poor souls never succeed in reaching the country of the dead.

"Now, during the short time that you are alive again, you will tell me about that path and its hazards. Together we will consider how these may be eased, or at least how the inexperienced ghost may be warned against them. Then, when the sun goes down, you will walk off into the west and again become one of the dead.

"From then on, you will be in charge of that dark trail. You will make the changes that we decide on. You will help the ghosts get safely through to their own country."

Nanabush spread sand on the stone and Tooth drew diagrams in it. He showed where the black bog crossed the path, and where the rushing river flowed under the serpent that looks like a log bridge. He heaped a little mound of sand for the hill where the strawberry tempts the traveller to a false turn. "Here sits the owl with the terrible eyes, and over here, the dog-monster."

They talked for the rest of the day. Then Tooth pushed the empty dish to Nanabush. "Keep this for me."

He crossed the hill to the west, and came out on the top of the next ridge. He turned there, and Nanabush could just hear his words. "Can you still see me?"

"Yes, I can see you, brother. And from now on, your name shall be He-walked-behind-the-Sunset."

In remembrance of him, we still give a dish to the wife, or child, or husband of someone who has died. That is called the mourning dish.

Woman and Serpent

When Leaves-blowing was thirteen she stopped being a little girl and became a woman. Her mother and her elder sister put a worn-out old dress on her and took her a long way over the lake to a tall island. On its summit there was a flat place sheltered from the wind by pines. There they made her a small lodge of poles and brush. They had brought no food for her but they did give her a stick to scratch any itch, for she must not touch herself with her hands. They blackened her face with charcoal and left her.

Leaves-blowing sat there for three days, looking out over the lake through an opening in the trees. On the fourth morning, when she was feeling quite faint from hunger, dark clouds came together and lightning flashed. She knew that the thunderers were speaking to her, but she could not make out their message. Then a gull came skimming over the waves. As it wheeled up before her she heard the words clearly.

"You are now blessed with power. Power of the thunder. Use it well and don't be afraid."

Leaves-blowing was happy. She had noticed some blueberry bushes near the water, and now she ate every berry she could find, even the little white ones. She scraped some lichen off a rock and ate that too, but not very much of it. Then she washed the black smudges off her face and sat down to wait some more.

Late the next morning she saw a canoe coming. She knew that her people would be in it and she walked out on a flat rock to meet them. As they came alongside she saw that the sister had her little boy tucked up in a padded place in the bow. Leaves-blowing leaned over him.

"Greetings, nephew. I am happy that you have come to take me away from this hungry place. And when we get back to the camp you can be one of the guests at my ceremony."

He looked up at her solemnly. The sister handed her a package wrapped in bark. Inside was a nicely-broiled whitefish. Leaves-blowing ate it and minded the baby while the other two limbered their legs in a walk along the shore.

When they came back, Leaves-blowing's mother looked at the sky. It was clear, and the wind was light and steady from the west. She stepped down into the center of the canoe, leaving the steersman's position in the stern empty. Leaves-blowing knelt there and took up the paddle, saying nothing, but proud to have this new responsibility.

Sister in the bow set a quick pace. They moved swiftly over the lake. Leaves-blowing looked at the cliffs along the coast and wondered what spirits might be watching from those high stony places. The thunderers lived even higher.

The noon sun beat down on the water and reflected up from it. Leaves-blowing's arms tired. She was glad each time that sister shifted sides with the paddle, allowing her to change too and to use a different set of muscles. But she kept a strong pressure on each stroke.

Suddenly, without the least warning, wind whipped around them. The flat lake wrinkled, then broke into raging waves. Leaves-blowing swung the canoe to meet them, shaking her head to get her blowing hair out of her eyes. They paddled up a rolling hill of green water, broke through the white froth at its top and seemed to pause there for just a moment before the steep rush down the other side.

In that instant Leaves-blowing, looking out over the lake, got a flash of some strange object that rose shining above the billows. On the next crest she saw it again, and quite clearly this time. It was the swaying head of a giant water-snake. A snake with antlers like a deer. She had never seen such a thing before, but she had heard of it. She knew that it was the child-stealer, Missikenabek, the great horned serpent.

The snake approached swiftly until it hung almost above them. The waves burst white against it and then dropped away, dripping from the gleaming rack of horns and pouring down the powerful pillar of the neck. Its voice came clear above the roar of the storm.

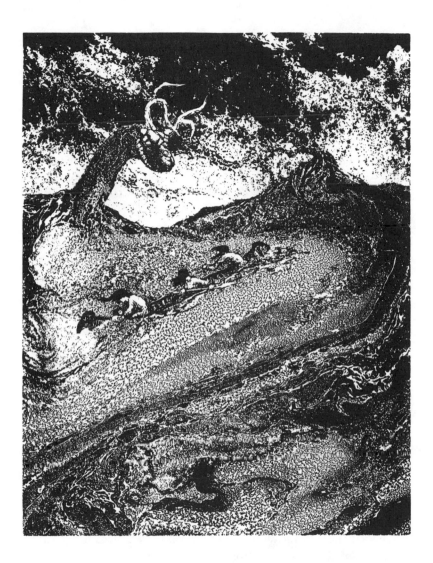

"I have no wish to harm you, my sisters. Just give me the baby. Then I will flatten the waters and you may go on your way."

The paddlers, struggling hard to surmount the waves and keep the canoe afloat, said nothing.

"I ask you for a small gift, something important to me that can't be of such great consequence to you. Don't be mean about it. Three fine, strong women like you can have many children. Surely you can spare me this one."

A fierce wave drove the canoe sideways in spite of Leaves-blowing's efforts. The next one broke over the gunwale. The mother-grandmother put down her paddle and bailed water quickly with a bark bucket. Working together, her daughters brought the canoe around to face into the wind again.

"You see, you can hardly stay right side up as it is. It would not be the least trouble for me to turn you over. Then you would drown and never have any more children. And I would get the baby anyway. It's all so simple and reasonable. Just toss him to me and go safely away with my thanks and blessing."

Leaves-blowing could see the long coil of his body creeping around them just below the surface, shining red up out of the green water. It was made of copper, just as the story-tellers had said.

"All right. I am not a waster. I don't like to destroy inedible animals. And I certainly don't consider stringy old hags like you edible. But reasoning with you is like arguing with rocks. Just remember, as you sink down to join the other boulders on the bottom, that you brought this on yourselves."

A thick, metallic length of tail slid out of the water and over the gunwale, feeling for a cross-brace. The older sister siezed the baby and bent over him. Her mother tried to push the tail away with her paddle. But it slithered on, found the thwart, curled around it, drew the canoe down on one side. The lake poured in.

The sky had grown dark with thunder clouds. A gull swooped low over Leaves-blowing. Maybe it spoke to her. She lifted her paddle high and swung it down with all her strength, like an axe, on the scaly tail.

There was a violent clap of thunder. The cedar blade did not splinter. It bit as though it had been made of steel. The tip of the tail fell, wriggling, and splashed into the water inside the canoe. Leaves-blowing could hear muffled, coppery clangs as it battered against the boat's ribs.

The serpent bellowed like a moose and plunged straight down into the lake. Instantly the wind died.

It seemed to take the waves a long time to subside. Even when the mother had bailed out the wallowing canoe it was heavy in the stern from the weight of the copper.

They paddled the rest of the distance as hard as they could. When Leaves-blowing looked back she could see only rolling swells, the aftermath of storm. But the serpent might be following below. They went on bending their paddles, pushing against the water.

When they came into the outlet where the camp was, the people were standing on the shore. Everybody had gathered to watch the approach of this strange craft, with its bow high in the air, driven with such terror that a curve of white water rushed out on each side.

Young men waded in, laid hands on the writhing tail and wrestled it out of the canoe. On the beach it shook them back and forth. Some were thrown, rolling across the sand, and one was sent splashing into the water. Others came running to help. By force of numbers they overcame it and half-dragged, half-carried it up close to the fire. There it seemed to gain new strength and lashed about so violently that they had to drop it.

It lay there, squirming, throughout Leaves-blowing's new-woman ceremony. The people stood well back from it at first but soon some grew bolder and at last even the most timid came and poked it.

At sunset it stopped wriggling. The mother beat out a piece of it and scratched a picture of the thunderers on it to make a sacred ornament. Leaves-blowing wore this all the rest of her life, hanging from a thong around her neck.

Her mother used more of the tail to make a bowl of copper. But there was still a big chunk of it left. The sister's husband took that to the trading post. The Saganash was delighted with it and gave him a beautiful shirt, a silver dollar, and many twists of tobacco.

From that time on he often took the baby back and forth over the long traverse between the river and the island. He carried an axe, out of sight from the water, in the bottom of the canoe. The boy liked those boat rides. He and his father used to paddle out there even when he was big, but he never saw the horns of Missikenabek lift out of the lake again.

The Swamp Lodge

Flint slipped the tump strap from his head, eased his pack to the ground, and rested the butt of the musket on a stump. The forest ended here.

He had been following this doe for two days. Her tracks had been the first sign of game that he had seen in a week.

She could not be far ahead now. The little heart-shaped footprints were crisp where a patch of snow still lay white in the shadow of a spruce thicket. Their edges had not yet begun to soften. Beyond the drift they disappeared into the scrubby vegetation of the swamp.

He could see no movement in that long waste of water and gray, winter-broken grass. A scattering of spruce stood up out of the flatness. Some were dead, some still showed scrawny clumps of green, but all were twisted into strange forms, stiff as the contorted limbs of drowned men. From their branches, streamers of dangling moss hung straight down. No breeze disturbed them, nor the surface of the dark pools. A solitary boulder floated above its reflection, the one as unwavering as the other.

It was said that the big bog was a witch-place. That might be so. It was certainly not safe walking. Flint had never ventured far into it and neither had any other hunter that he knew. And he was tired.

He was very tired, but, even more than tired, he was hungry. He hoisted his burdens and followed the tracks, stepping carefully.

The earth, what there was of it, was sodden with melting snow and with the invasions of flooding ponds and streams. It quaked at every step, and ripples ran out through it, shaking tufts of grass and distant bushes.

A hummock might look solid, even feel firm to a trial foot-push, but still give way under a man's full weight. That could tilt the hunter into an icy pool, up to his armpits or deeper.

He made the kill when the gray sky was darkening and the outer surfaces of his waterlogged leggings and moccasins were beginning to freeze. He thanked the deer quickly, gutted her, lifted her to his shoulders, and splashed on, looking for high ground.

He found it as the last light faded, a flat island of worn-down stone. The load was getting heavy. He pushed through the dense belt of shoreline bushes and climbed over a tangle of fallen timber.

Under the canopy of standing trees the small brush thinned. Flint came to a sudden stop. Just ahead, clearly visible between the trunks of a clump of jackpines, was a bark wigwam. A gleam of firelight flickered, for a moment, at the smokehole.

He wondered whether this might be the camp of a war party, a base, in this remote spot, for an attack on his people. None of the Anishinabeg would be camping here. But the 'Bwaneg, the hated roasters, were even farther away and this was not their kind of lodge.

He eased the carcass down, and then the pack. There were some traps inside and a chain clinked as it settled to the ground.

Flint froze, the musket covering the wigwam. There was no sound or movement there. He walked quietly forward, bent at the entrance, and swept up the doorskin.

A woman sat by the fire. She smiled a welcome, showing two large front teeth that enhanced, rather than diminished, the calm beauty of her finely modelled face. She leaned to one side and rolled out a robe over the spruce bedding beside her.

Flint stood still at the doorway. His gun was not pointed at her, but not far from her either. A bushwoman could be even more dangerous than a 'Bwan. But no, looking at her closely he knew that this was neither an enemy nor an evil spirit. He put down the musket and lowered himself gratefully upon the fur.

"There is meat out there," he said.

She hung a kettle over the flame, took a knife, and went out. Flint dozed a while and was wakened by the smell and gurgle of simmering venison. The woman had taken off her moccasins and was warming her feet.

She set the kettle before him. He speared a chunk with his knife, cut a piece off, and handed it to her.

"You eat the deer," she said. "I like this better."

She reached back under the dark edge of the wigwam, drew out something that looked like a piece of aspen, and began to gnaw at it. By the time he had finished the stew she had eaten the twigs, buds, and all the bark.

"Each one to his taste," said Flint. "But now I have three questions to ask you. What is wrong with your feet, what is your name, and will you be my wife?"

"My feet are a little different from yours. Like this."

She spread her toes and he could see that they were long and had webs between them.

"There is nothing wrong with them. They are all the better to swim with. The answers to your other two questions are Sedgeflower and yes.

"But one thing you must promise me. You must never again kill a beaver."

"I dearly love beaver. And the trader pays well for the pelts."

They sat silent for a while. He was thinking of all the good things that came from beaver, but he was also watching the firelight glint on her broad cheeks and glossy hair.

"All right," he said. "I suppose that the animal is your vision-protector and that any harm done to it might bring misfortune on you. I will kill no more beaver."

Sedgeflower proved to be a good wife. She cooked well, kept the lodge clean and the clothing mended, brought in plenty of firewood, and was the best woman Flint had ever known at finding edible plants, roots and berries.

She also turned out to be something of a healer. When he fell and broke a finger she set it, splinted it in cedar strips and said a short but effective incantation over it so that he was soon able to use it again.

He set his traps where they would not be likely to take beaver. Even so, sometimes one did get caught. Then he held it down with a forked stick, being careful neither to injure it nor to let it bite him, while he stepped on the spring of the trap to drop the steel jaws away from the foot.

In the late autumn he took what furs he had trapped and went back across the frozen bog. He stayed several days in Broken Sky's lodge while they waited for the Indian trader with the dog team and the long toboggan loaded with white-man goods from the south.

When the exchange was finished, Broken Sky invited Flint to hunt with him that winter. His wife had inherited a particularly rich meat and fur territory up on the Wenadaga. They would be glad to have him as a partner.

"It cannot be good to live so far away in the great bog. Something will happen to you there. Go back and get the woman, if you want her, and then join us."

"She is a swamp person. She would not be happy in high country."

He bound his sacks and boxes with a tumpline, slipped the strap over his head, leaned forward to hoist the load, and went back to the swamp lodge.

When it came time for Sedgeflower to give birth, Flint did what he could for her. She didn't seem to need much help, though. The baby slipped out easily, and then another. When a third appeared, Flint's jaw dropped open. But then he saw still another shiny little head push into the firelight.

Two boys and two girls. Strong, healthy children that grew fast. They had their mother's teeth and feet, but in other respects they took after their father. He was proud and amazed to see them, in a few weeks, running over the muskeg and swimming in the ponds and river. By the time they were two years old they were all helping with the work. The boys did not seem much interested in hunting, but that would come later.

One evening, on a trail far from the home lodge, Flint found a large beaver caught in one of his traps. For a moment he stood, drooling a little, as he admired the fine fat tail.

Then he sighed and turned away. He cut a stout birch sapling, trimmed it to a crotch, and forced the animal firmly to the ground. The stick slipped against the muddy bank. The man fell forward, coming down on the beaver whose foot was still held in the trap. The big curved teeth slashed, ripped a forearm to the bone. Flint struck in blind fury, bringing the butt of the pole down with all his strength.

He sprang to his feet and stepped back, but the fight was over. The beaver kicked a little and lay quiet.

Flint bound up the torn arm. "You can't say that was my fault."

The beaver did not answer.

"Well, you're dead. I can't bring you back to life and nothing I do to you now will make you any deader. I don't know what bad luck you will bring, but you may as well do me some good."

He skinned the carcass. The trader would give a lot of lead and powder for that fine pelt. No, he would get print material, ribbons, and a mirror.

It was too late to think of going any farther that night. He built a fire, cut the tail into strips, and roasted them on sticks. It tasted good, but did not make him happy.

He didn't sleep much and got up as soon as early light showed him the way. There was still quite a lot of beaver, but he left it for whatever animal might happen along. That was one kind of meat that he was not going to carry home.

When he reached the lodge he found it empty. Tracks led down to a river in the marsh. He searched far upstream and down but could find no trace of their having left the water on either bank.

It was hard to believe that five good swimmers had all drowned. And yet the tracks could not lie. Not in that soft mud.

He had done wrong last night, and this must be the punishment.

He ran along the bank, splashing through the pools, falling and shouting like a drunken man. When a slough barred his path he plunged into it and went down in the soft black, liquid muck.

He struggled, felt the swamp clutch at his feet, dragging him deeper.

Then a strong, live thing was beneath his chin, pushing up, lifting his face above the surface. A familiar voice spoke close to his ear.

"Over here, father."

He stretched out his hand toward the sound. The wildly grasping fingers closed on something solid. He pulled himself to it, blowing hard, and wiped the mud and slime out of his eyes. When he could see again, he found that he was clinging to a tree trunk. He heard more words.

"Mother dropped the popple there. She left the bark attached to the stump and told me to stay here, and watch for you. She always plans things well, but I don't see how she knew you'd stumble into this hole. You're usually so cautious."

Flint looked over the water and up the shore. No person was in sight, but a beaver's head moved through the water near him. Its mouth opened. It was talking.

"Don't you know me, father? My mother and your wife, Sedgeflower, has been waiting for you at the lodge all morning."

Flint pulled himself up a little farther.

"That can't be," he thought, but he hadn't enough breath to say anything.

He hung silently to the log for a while, then spoke in short gasps.

"I just came from the lodge . . .

"My wife wasn't there . . ."

He spat out some waterlogged leaves.

"Nor any of the children . . ."

"Oh, you mean the old bark house on the land," said the beaver. "We don't live there any more. It wouldn't be safe, what with the lynx around, and other varmints."

"Well I'm not going to argue about it any longer here."

Slowly, careful now, he dragged himself along the poplar. When he reached solid ground he sat down on the trunk. As soon as he had his breath he spoke firmly.

"Now, what's all this about your mother being my wife. I don't think that I like that kind of talk."

The beaver popped up again from the river.

"Well, then, as you said, let's not argue about it here. She can explain it better than I. The bottom is firm on this side. Just walk in and follow me."

Flint slid down the bank, waded into the stream and felt his way after the slow-paddling beaver. There were no more sink holes, but he was soon over his depth and swimming.

His guide led him around a grassy point, up a tributary creek and over a dam to a broad expanse of water. On the far side was wooded benchland. He saw, in the wavering reflection of the trees, a beaver sitting on a large stick-and-mud lodge watching them.

"Come here, Flint," she called. "I am Sedgeflower and there are things that I have to tell you."

He thrashed across the calm water of the pond and clambered up beside her.

"Is it really you, my wife?"

He reached out to her, but she moved away.

"You have done the forbidden deed. I sent for you so that you would know that we are well even though we have changed. And so that you would not go plowing up the bog looking for us. Now it will be best that you go back to your own people."

"You are my own people. I will be just like one of you. I will never hurt another beaver."

An old head with white whiskers popped up out of the water.

"Is he safe, daughter?"

"I cannot promise that. He doesn't always keep his word. You had better be careful."

"I will do you no harm," said Flint. "I don't want to go back to men. Let me stay here with you and live as you live."

The old beaver floated, his tail and hind paws moving just enough to hold him in position against the light current.

"I believe that your intentions are good and I would like to help you. But I wonder how it would work out. What do you think, daughter?"

Sedgeflower brought up a hind foot and rubbed her chin thoughtfully.

"We beavers are fond of men. We pity them when they starve and we befriend them. They could not live out a winter if it were not for the furs and fat meat that we give them.

"This one is not bad as people go. I suppose I would take him back if you think we should keep him and if he shows himself worthy. But a man is only a man. He cannot be expected to behave like a beaver.

"He has killed and he may kill again. He would not work as we work. He does not always keep himself clean. He would probably go sniffing after other females. Those are the unfortunate weaknesses of humans.

"And he doesn't care for the sweet green popple bark. How about that, husband?"

"My mind is made up. I will stay with you. I will eat what you eat."

A plump little beaver scrambled gracefully up the side of the lodge. Her eyes were bright and her fur was a warm chestnut-brown.

"Greetings, brother-in-law. I think that you should stay. I will dig up sweet roots for you and duck-potatoes from the bottom of the slough."

"Keep out of this, Sundrop," said Sedgeflower. "Let him decide for himself. I will not be a wife to him again unless and until he has proved that he can act like one of us."

By this time the whole colony was watching from the water and from the bank. An old female spoke.

"He is the father of my grandchildren. It would not be proper for me to say anything to him, but you tell him, Birch-cutter, that he can stay in my lodge."

"In that case," said the white-whiskered grandfather, "it will need some alterations. So now we had better get to work."

Instantly the surface of the water was cut by spreading wakes as beavers churned off for sticks to plaster on the outside of the house. Others gnawed out more space in the main room and widened the entrance.

When all was ready, Sedgeflower dived and Flint followed her down through the dark water, into the submerged passage.

This had seemed plenty wide to the beavers but was still narrow to a broad-shouldered man. Too narrow for swimming. He dragged himself along, gripping and pulling on the sides.

Finally these walls came so close together that he could no longer get his hands up past his body. The great effort was swiftly exhausting the air supply in his lungs.

He squirmed a little farther, then could make no more progress. He tried to back up, and found that impossible. The

thought flashed across his mind that he would drown here like a beaver in a sliding trap-set.

Sedgeflower turned, braced her hind feet against the sides of the tunnel, got her forepaws under his chin, and pulled. Flint struggled desperately. They began to make a little headway. At that moment Birchcutter swam in behind him and gave a strong shove.

The sides of the passage reluctantly loosened their grip. Flint came to the surface in the the dark central chamber. He crawled out on an earth platform. He lay there, panting, on a mattress of shredded willow bark while the family enlarged the narrow place.

The space into which he had emerged was some ten feet long and half as wide. Its walls had been cut smooth by the chisel teeth. This was the living room. There was a separate bedroom, a dining room over another plungehole, and a toilet room. This last was cleaned regularly. But every part of the lodge was kept spotless.

It took Flint several days to summon enough courage to try the outward passage, but when he did there was no further trouble.

Everybody was busy getting in a plentiful supply of food. Most of the work was done at night. Saplings and brush were piled in a deep part of the pond near the lodge where they would be available all winter. The gnawed points were pushed into the mud and stones were laid on the tops and branches to anchor the growing mass.

Flint helped, carrying poles and brush that the beavers had cut. At dusk or by moonlight he hauled big armfuls along the tote-roads that they had laid out to the canals that ran out from the water. There wasn't much he could do on dark nights but he was able to convince himself, and maybe his in-laws, that he was making a substantial contribution to the effort. At least he didn't have to drop everything and dive into the water every time a tail-slap warned of an approaching predator.

Sundrop was diligent in searching the river bottom for delicacies. For a time, he found these quite adequate. But after a few weeks, he felt the grip of the meat-hunger. And of love-hunger, too.

Sedgeflower had meant what she said. When he approached her affectionately she spoke firm words.

"You are not yet one of us. I will wait another month and see how you shape up. Then I will decide whether to take you back."

At bedtime, after one hard night's work, he walked up to to the edge of the logging area and sat there under the trees, looking out over the river flats beyond the pond and reflecting on the fickle nature of women.

There was a stirring in the brush at his side and he turned to find that his sister-in-law had sought him out to bring him some particularly succulent rush roots.

"Why Sundrop, you shouldn't come so far from the water."

"I am not afraid of any lynx or wolf when you are with me."

She was beautiful there in the warming sunlight.

He ate the roots, wishing that they were moose muffle. She sat beside him, combing her hair with the long serrated inner claws of a hind foot, and reaching back, from time to time, for a footfull of rich, musky oil to work into it.

This perfume had a prompt and powerful effect on Flint. He stroked the long, iridescent back-hair, then pushed his nose down into the underfur and inhaled. He came out of those enchanting depths like a swimmer rising from a deep dive. He sought her mouth. She opened furry lips to him. That morning, one of his hungers was satisfied.

They returned to their secluded spot the next day, and again. The others must have noticed how late they were coming into the lodge, and the females might have talked about it. Flint and Sundrop didn't care. Let them gossip!

All through each sweating night, he thought about her and about the delights of daybreak's romantic rendezvous. What if Sedgeflower wouldn't take him back. He was doing all right.

It disturbed him, though, that his emotions were shifting. He was as eager for Sundrop as ever. But now that his erotic desire was being so capably fulfilled, the other carnal lust was becoming more demanding.

When he caressed her beautiful tail, his hand, instead of hastening on to those demesnes that there adjacent lay, lingered lovingly on its scaly surface. He was no longer anticipating amorous ecstacy. He was thinking of the broad, fat, paddle-shaped appendage itself and how it would taste roasted.

One morning, after a dawn tryst, neither of the lovers returned to the lodge. Three days passed. Then, as the family sat together in the living room, Flint's head broke the surface of the plunge-hole and he crawled out alone.

He went directly to Birchcutter.

"I don't know just how to tell you this, sir."

The old beaver waited in polite silence.

"I have eaten your younger daughter. I'm sorry. I doubt that this will help, but I will say that she was delicious. A dish for the manedog."

"What did you do with her bones?"

"I picked each of them clean and then I threw them into the bushes."

Birchcutter was unable to conceal his displeasure.

"You have not been well brought up. I suppose none of you are, these days. The old-time people treated our bones with respect.

"Go back now and collect them. Be sure to find every one. Put them into running water. Then return here."

Flint tried to do as he had been told, laying out each of the pieces in its proper place. It wasn't easy. The little animal-folk had been working on the bones and had scattered them over a considerable area. He persisted and at last had the complete skeleton, except a small toe-bone from the left hind foot.

He looked for it a long time, pushing bushes aside, sifting through dead leaves and turning over the wooden chips of the beaver cuttings. The day was hot and the flies were biting. Finally he gave up, put the bones into a cedar bark bag, and set out for the river.

He was worried about the missing part, but he didn't feel that it was altogether his fault.

"The father should have told me about that custom before instead of after. Then I would have saved them all."

He emptied the bag into the water where the current was swift, and went back to the pond.

Before the next dawn, all the beavers stopped work and assembled around the lodge. The water was glassy still, black in the shore reflections except where masses of lilies, still closed for the night, lay pale across it.

Flint thought he heard a faint splash as though something had slipped from the dam. The lilies began to waver, a shifting string of pale dots against the darkness. Then he saw a bright ever-widening ripple that came swiftly over the water toward them. At the point of the vee he made out a head followed by a strip of glossy back. It was Sundrop.

She had some difficulty in getting up the side of the lodge. She was limping, steadying herself with her tail.

She only glanced at Flint but that short look would have burned the lichen off a boulder.

Sedgeflower examined the weak leg and foot, then shook her head, frowning.

"I have never seen this kind of an injury. The skin is not broken and yet one of the toe-bones is missing. I cannot understand it."

"I can," said Birchcutter. "Now, Flint, you must leave us. But remember what you have learned here.

"We were bigger than bears once, but we were always good to humans. The Indians were grateful to us then, and ever since, until the white man came. Now they seem to think that they are something special and that all the other animals have been made for their benefit.

"If you want us to keep on putting fur on your backs and meat in your bellies you must go back to the old ways.

"Never speak ill of a beaver. Make us offerings of tobacco at proper intervals. Count the number of heads in each lodge and take only the surplus, no matter how much the trader is paying for pelts.

"The hunting and trapping must be done decently. That means only at the cold time when the people need meat and the fur is prime. And always it must be followed with the full thank-you ceremonies.

"Do not give even one of our bones to the dogs, but put them all back in the water. That makes it possible for us to rise from the dead, as you have seen.

"Remember these things and tell them to your people.

"That is all."

He struck the water with his tail. There was a staccato answer of slaps as every beaver dived.

After a while Sedgeflower came out on the lodge. Sundrop followed, crawling painfully up over the mass of sticks and mud to sit beside her. Together they watched the man grow small and finally disappear in the shadows and the stunted trees of the big bog.

The Windigos

I will tell you about what happened in the hungry winter, that year when the rice was dry and thin, and the deer went away, and the fish were unwilling to be caught.

The men hunted all day and the women dug in the earth trying to find enough things that could be eaten to keep body and shadow together. But when the rivers froze, the little death-bird flew down and perched above the wigwam.

In such winters, the cannibal windigos come walking out of the woods, pretending to be men, but all the time looking for their favorite meat. When three of them came up here into the high country, Rain-from-the-Northeast wrapped himself in the sacred skin of a white bear. Then he fought them. He shot two of them and they turned into wolverines and died. The other one went back into the bush. After that, the people were able to starve in peace.

But by the lakes a big windigo pulled down the burial scaffolds and dug up the graves. When there were no more dead he ate the living. When he ran out of Indians he went south and ate the Saganash.

The soldiers' rifles couldn't kill him, nor even their wagon-guns. The king of Michigan sent for a wise medicine man and asked his advice.

"Nothing can stop this windigo," he said, "except another windigo. I do not know how you can recruit one. I suggest that you send for Rain-from-the-Northeast, who knows more about these matters than any other man."

The king thanked him and did as he advised.

At Bawating, the medicine line runs deep under the water where you cannot see it. That is so far south that the rapids were still open, even then in the moon of little ghosts. But the smooth river below them was frozen, and Rain-from-the-Northeast walked across the ice from the grandmother's country into Michigan, the land of the big-knives.

The king was waiting for him. They sat and smoked together, but only for a short time. Then the king spoke.

"The windigo has stopped all logging operations. He is much bigger than your little northern windigos. Bullets bounce off him. We are afraid that when he finishes at the camps he will go on to Detroit. If you kill him, or arrange for him to die, I will give you half my kingdom and the hand of my daughter, the Princess Sylvia, in marriage. Here she is."

"How do you do," said the princess.

Rain-from-the-Northeast walked around her, looking at her front, back, and sideways. When he had finished he stood rubbing his nose. Finally he turned to the king.

"It's too bad she isn't heavier. But I will kill your windigo anyway.

"I will take the woman now. Not just her hand—that wouldn't do me any good. I will take all of her." He handed her a pair of snowshoes and a caribou robe. "But I don't want any part of Michigan."

"No deal," said the king. "I won't give you Sylvia or anything else until the windigo is dead."

But Rain-from-the-Northeast was already walking off across the snow. The princess stood watching him for a few moments. Then she tied on the snowshoes, wrapped herself in the robe and followed him. They went over the frozen river into Canada.

She wasn't much good at first. Rain-from-the-Northeast told her to build a lodge, but the wind blew it down. He had to help her set up a strong frame, cover it with bark and reinforce it with treetrunks. Then he showed her how to cut wood and carry it in with a tump line. And other things about living in the winter woods.

She wasn't lazy or stupid, but she didn't know anything. He spent several days teaching her before he felt that he could leave her alone in camp.

On the second day of hunting he killed a caribou. He showed Sylvia how to skin and cut up the carcass, put the fat into a copper kettle, and render it into grease, and pour it into birch bark pails. Then he hurried on and in the next week he killed two more caribou and a bear.

He gave most of the meat to some people. They could hardly believe that he had found deer and bear in that empty forest. Sylvia wrapped the grease pails into packs. Then they started south.

When they came to the river they saw the king waiting on the American side.

"What took you so long?" he asked. "There are hardly any loggers left."

"Everything in good time, father-in-law," said Rain-from-the-Northeast. "Where is the windigo?"

"Here he comes now," said the king as he stepped behind a boulder.

There was the roar and rush of stormy wind and the pop of breaking treetrunks.

"Start a fire, wife," said Rain-from-the-Northeast, "and then do as I told you."

He opened a pack, took out the sacred bearskin, and swung it around his shoulders. He began to grow, and the skin grew with him. Twice the size of an ordinary man and an ordinary white bear, three times. But he was no longer an ordinary man. He was a windigo.

The other windigo was even bigger. His face looked like the skull of Pauguk. The eyes were holes in the head and he had chewed away his own lips so that you could see all his teeth. He tore up a great red pine and swung it around his head. The stones and frozen chunks of dirt went hurtling out from its roots.

The Rain-from-the-Northeast windigo ducked and the flying fragments crashed into the brush. He grabbed a live pine, jerked hard, but the roots held in the frozen ground. Dodging, he came on a dead tree, but big and sound. He broke it off and part of its stump came with it. When the giant brought the pine down at him he turned the blow with its trunk.

The fight swayed back and forth through the forest. It left a churning-up of snow in clouds like a blizzard and a trail of broken timber like a tornado. The princess built a fire, set up

a tripod of green logs over it, and hung the copper kettle by a chain from where they came together. She filled this with chunks of grease. She could hear the crashing of battle in the distance.

She stirred the kettle and licked the nice rich stuff off her horn spoon. After a while she poked the burning wood apart leaving just enough fire to keep the grease hot.

At noon everything got quiet. The king peeked out from behind his rock and then came over and held his hands to the fire.

"Put on more wood, daughter, and give me some of that soup that smells so good."

She filled a bowl with the melted fat and handed it to him.

"Let it cool a little, father, or it will burn your mouth."

He soon took a sip, waited a while, took more, and then quickly drank all the grease and scraped the bowl. But when he heard trees breaking in the forest again he hurried back behind his boulder.

This time the noise approached more slowly. Sylvia put more wood on the fire, heating up the grease until it bubbled nicely. Rain-from-the-Northeast came backing out of the brush, straining and grunting as he dragged the body of the other windigo.

He laid it out beside the fire.

"Where is the axe?" he asked. "This is a kind of manedo. We must get the heart out of him quickly before he comes back to life."

Sylvia ran to where she had been cutting wood, and came back with the axe. Rain-from-the-Northeast had to swing hard because windigos are ice inside even while they are alive. Chips flew in all directions.

At last he held the big, frozen heart in his hands. He reached it out over the kettle and dropped it in, stepping back quickly so as not to get spattered.

The grease stopped bubbling, but Sylvia had plenty of wood ready, and put on more until it boiled again. The king thought that she looked small beside her gigantic husband. He decided to stay behind the boulder.

Rain-from-the-Northeast sat resting and looking away from his wife so that he would not have to eat her. Then he got up, cut a forked maple, and used it as tongs to fish out the heart. It was still frozen inside, so he put it back into the kettle and looked away.

The king was almost frozen himself by this time. He crept out and sat close to the fire and Sylvia. When Rain-from-the-Northeast turned around again it was almost dark. But now the heart was thawed and he ate it. The princess began to pull the logs apart.

"Leave a little fire there," he said. "I'm not finished with it yet."

He swung the kettle up, letting the chain dangle while he took a swig. He drank quite a lot, then set it back over the coals. "Put some more fat in, wife," he said. Soon he grew smaller.

He went on like that, lapping the grease and heating it up again. He turned to the others.

"How am I now?"

"You'd better take some more."

He drank a lot more. Sylvia was keeping the kettle full, and watching her husband closely. After a while she spoke.

"Stand up and let me look at you."

He got to his feet.

"I'd say take some more," said the king.

Rain-from-the-Northeast stood holding the bucket and watching his wife.

"That's about it, right now," she said. "I'm glad that I'm no longer married to a windigo, but I wouldn't want you to get too little."

He set down the bucket and she scraped the rest of the grease back into the bark pails.

She had made a lean-to of poles and spruce boughs near the fire and had piled snow on it with her snowshoes to keep the wind from blowing through it. They slept there that night.

In the morning the king invited them to live at Lansing.

"I will give you a wing of the palace. You will have more room there than in a wigwam, and servants to bring you breakfast. There are fountains, and dancers, and wine, and an orchestra plays soft music at dinner."

"Thank you, father-in-law. I would like to see that place. But the winter is not over. The people need meat, and other windigos may come out of the bush. Perhaps when the ice breaks we will paddle down and visit you."

And again they walked back across the river.

Dance of the Seasons

Bexie knelt on the rock landing and pushed the bucket down. It was big, made of birch bark, round at the top, broadening to a square bottom. The water surged in and over it, chilling her hands. She dragged it up by its leather harness and rested it, sagging and dripping on the stone, while she tied the cover in place.

She grunted a little as she hoisted it to her back, feeling her feet spread out and press down through her moccasins against the granite. Then she was walking, leaning forward with most of the weight on her hips, searching her way up the dark trail.

She took the steep place on hands and knees, paying no attention to the bite of the rock beneath. But she stopped twice to loosen and jerk free from the spruce twigs that came sneaking in, stiff and eager as old men's fingers, to grasp her hair.

She was breathing hard when she came out into the firelight. Beside the ledge she turned, tilted her head back, and slipped the strap off slowly to lower the sloshing burden without spilling any more than she had to. She straightened up, wriggled her shoulders, and came over to the fire, standing close to it, warming her back, drying her dress, and enjoying the sweet birch smoke.

"You should be more careful," said Unzig. "There is no need to waste water and soak yourself like that."

She held a flare of burning bark over the bucket and peered down into it. Then she pulled up her sleeve, reached in, chased something slippery, caught it, held it out to Sawbill. He continued to gaze into the fire.

111

"See, husband."

He inspected her exhibit briefly, then turned back to the flame. "Yes," he said. "It's a clear night. A little ice is freezing around the shore. It will go away when the sun comes."

"It will go away, husband, but it will not stay away. It will come back tomorrow night. Soon it will spread out over the lake and cut us off from the world until the birch buds swell. We have lived almost a year on this steep and lonely rock where we cannot see the opposite shore and where we never meet anybody who doesn't have fins."

Sawbill frowned.

"Do not speak slightingly of those who wear fins. We are close to the cove here and they might hear you. It's not a nice way to talk, anyway, about friends who have been kind to us."

"Oh, I'm grateful to them. The racks are bending with trout and whitefish. We could make gifts to many people and still have enough for the winter."

She stopped, watching him closely. He said nothing and she went on.

"The giving and the thanksgiving ceremonies will be starting soon at Rat Root. Let us paddle down there and take our part. Then we will come home happy and the snow will not seem so deep nor the wind so cold."

"The gathering at the river is not a good place for chaste women," Sawbill said firmly. "I have completely forgotten what happened there last year. So, of course, I will not speak of it now."

"That was not my fault. Bexie made me do it. I told you not to marry that sloppy little flirt. But I know what to watch for now. I will keep her in line. This time you will have nothing to worry about."

"All right, yes," said Sawbill. "Yes, we will go. And yes, this time I will have nothing to worry about. I intend to make sure of that. Put another log on, Bexie."

The younger wife moved quickly. Sawbill waited while the sparks spiraled upward and the new wood settled comfortably for the burning.

"This time, Unzig, there will be no crude behavior. Neither of you will have anything to do with the young men. Especially, you will not speak to Loon.

"And that's not all. We will eat the opening feast together. But when the dancing begins, you and Bexie will go to my mother's lodge and stay with her."

Unzig got up and stood tall above him. Her words rasped like a chipped file on a rusty musket barrel.

"I will not have that old owl sitting beside the door with her big round eyes watching my every move while you are flying around with the fledglings."

"That's unfair, and you know it. I'm not interested in other women."

Unzig's eyes narrowed as she inhaled audibly and ominously.

Sawbill went on quickly. "Not any more."

He could feel the dark word-cloud hanging over his head, held back in growing fury, but ready to burst into flood. He went on quickly.

"I am perfectly content with you and Bexie. I will dance, and smoke a while with the men, and I will drink a little, and then I will come back to you."

"If you're going to dance, so am I. I will roost on the rocks no longer. I must stretch my flight feathers."

"Very well," said Sawbill. "In that case we will all stay here on our headland and get in more wood. Which is just what we ought to be doing anyway."

He put his pipe back in his mouth and stared hard at the fire. She stood above him, rigid, saying nothing, but giving no ground.

A breath of wind fluttered the flame and swirled a few dead leaves into the mutinous silence. Bexie caught Unzig's eye and signaled with a little jerk of her head. The two women went out into the darkness.

When they came back, the first wife sank down cross-legged in her place beside Sawbill.

"I have decided to do as you think best, husband. We will stay in the mother-in-law's wigwam while you dance."

In the clean chill of dawn, Sawbill stood in the opening between the spruce trees. Below, the trail fell away to the the circle of the cove, sheltered from the long glitter of 'Tschgumi by guardian points of boulder and pine. Above and behind him rose the peaks and palisades of the shore range, stretching south in a series of sawteeth that got smaller and smaller until they disappeared in distant mists. As far as he knew, this lake and those mountains went on forever.

Somewhere, though, far down that coast, the barrier was broken by the valley of the Rat Root. There the people would now be gathering to erect the pole and bark lodges of a great, beautiful, dangerous village. There they would feast, chant, pray, dance, and be grateful for a few nights and then would fade back into the forest, leaving only trampled grass and frozen refuse.

He swung the canoe to his shoulders and carried it down the path, one hand holding a cross-brace, the other feeling for steadying grips on trees and boulders. He walked slowly, giving his moccasins time to find firm holds in the ice-slippery stone. On the flat rocks of the landing he lowered the boat to one knee and then to the water. Unzig held it floating while Bexie packed it with fish gifts, rolled bedding, and the small things that they would need as visitors. She left openings in the stern and in the bow, but there was no place for a passenger in the middle. Sawbill looked his question.

"We have a full load. Your second wife will go separately."

Bexie was already undressing. She wrapped her clothes and moccasins into a compact bundle and handed it to Unzig. Then she ran up the slant of a boulder and sailed off it in a long, flat dive, aimed far out so as not to hit the rim of ice.

She was a strong swimmer. By the time the canoe was under way she was just a dark spot in the shimmering distance. They had to paddle hard to keep her in sight.

At noon she waited for them, floating lightly, arms and legs spread just below the surface, her eyes closed.

"Wake up, lazy one," Unzig called, "we're here. What have you got for us to eat?"

Bexie opened her eyes, swirled up out of the water, arching her body forward, and then plunged down so that her feet followed the curve and her toes disappeared last.

They did not see her again for a long time. Then she came up with a herring in her mouth. She tossed it into the canoe where it flopped and bounced in front of Sawbill. She dived again, and brought up another for Unzig.

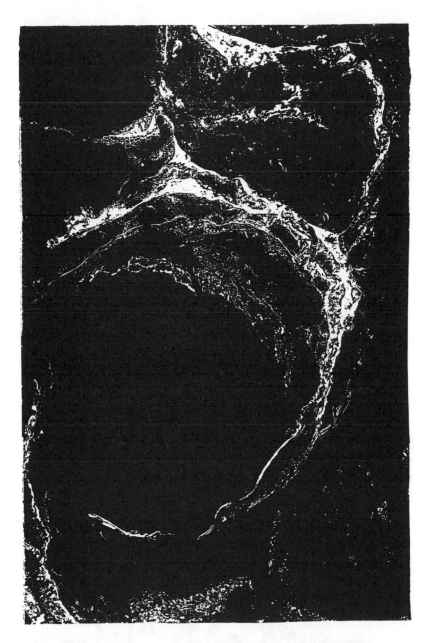

The first wife grabbed hers with one hand, turned it head foremost, and swallowed it without interrupting her paddle rhythm. "Now we won't have to land for tea," she called back. "Bexie wants time to polish her plumage before we get into town."

At sunset they found her squatting on the long point that almost closes the mouth of the Rat Root. She pulled the bow up a little, slantwise to the shore. Unzig tossed the bundle of clothing to her, took her own pack, and stepped out on the sand. She bathed quickly, shuddering at the cold water, pulled on wide, brightly-beaded leggings, and drew a dress over her head—a rich ceremonial garment of dark broadcloth. As they dressed the two women glanced down into the lake from time to time, making their adjustments from the reflections. They helped each other with their hair. When they had finished, their heads gleamed with a reddish sheen.

Sawbill had been squatting patiently on the beach. Now they greased his coarse black crest, combed it, rubbed some spots out of his jacket, painted his face, and tied an elaborately ornamented sash around his waist. Then they stepped back and looked at him. Bexie kicked at the sand and made a mouth.

"Well, it's the best we can do," said Unzig. "We or anybody else."

They paddled around the point with Bexie perched on the fish. Not really a stable load, but safe enough in the quiet water of evening.

As they approached the village they could see many canoes on the bank. Domed lodges glowed warm beyond the cooking fires. Nearer to the water, figures were moving about, dark against the flickering light. One of these, a big one, came wading out and grasped the gunwale. He spoke in a loud voice, as though the canoe were still out on 'Tschgumi.

"Greetings, Brother Sawbill, and welcome to Rat Root City. I have been eagerly awaiting you and your lovely ladies. You are just in time for dinner. I will help you ashore. But first, here, drink this."

"No thanks, Loon," said Sawbill. "And don't bother about the unloading. The women will take care of that."

But Loon was already carrying the packs across the beach. He kicked an inquisitive dog out of the way and held up a whitefish, patting, squeezing, and talking to it.

"Welcome to you too, you flat and smoky beauty. You and your companions are fortunate among fishes. You will be the most honored gifts of the festival. Not only for your own delicious virtues, but also for those of the wonderful women who have so daintily split, gutted and dried you."

"Please stop flattering my fish and my wives," said Sawbill. "They're adequate, but not that unusual. I don't want any of them spoiled. I ask that you now go somewhere else."

Loon smiled, whispered something to Bexie, and walked gracefully away, leaving an aroma of forgiveness for Sawbill's churlish manner and of sympathy for his wives.

Owl came hobbling up, took the pipe out of her mouth, and threw her arms around Sawbill. She greeted her daughters-in-law graciously, trying hard, but not with complete success, to hide her contempt for them.

The speeches of gratitude were beginning: to the plants, animals, birds, and fishes that had presented themselves in such abundance; to the rocks, trees, and waters that had been their home; and to each of the manedog—the spirits, good and evil—that control the destinies of living and unliving things.

It was a long list, and care was taken that none should be overlooked. But the dinner of duck, venison, wild rice, and delicately flavored roots, with wild ginger, wild onion, and maple sugar, was all the more appreciated. The Sawbill family's trout and whitefish were honored and enjoyed.

Everyone ate until they could hold no more. At this season, when bears and people had better store what fat they can in their bodies, gluttony is not a sin.

At the end of the feast the guests lay torpid around the fires, looking as though nothing could arouse them. Then a drum began to throb. Sawbill raised himself on an elbow, belched, and turned to Owl.

"Now, mother, it is time for you and the wives to leave. They have had a long journey. They will need sleep."

Owl watched her charges closely as she shepherded them along the trail. When Bexie stepped aside into an alder thicket she hooted at her.

"It's all right, mother," said Unzig. "It's just that she was drinking so much of that maple sugar tea."

"It's not all right," screeched Owl.

She flew into the darkness. There was some threshing about among the kinky little trunks, and then she came out with Bexie clutched in her claws. They were followed by a wierd laugh from the bush.

Bexie walked the rest of the way with an erratic, spread-legged stride. Unzig heard a gurgle from time to time, but Owl, having retrieved the errant daughter-in-law, seemed to be satisfied. Back in her home lodge, she was in no particular hurry.

"Speaking of tea," she said, "I always take a little before I go to bed. I couldn't sleep without my tea."

She hung a kettle over the fire while the girls selected places on the spruce bough bedding and laid out their sleeping gear. Unzig had a heavy red point blanket, symbol of the senior wife. Bexie's covering was an old robe of caribou hides.

"You rest, mother dear," said Unzig. "Bexie's good with tea."

Owl lay back on the spruce. Unzig stood between her and Bexie. The second wife reached under her skirt, her hands busy, untying something. At the same time she was peeking around Unzig, never taking her eyes off the mother-in-law. Still watching, she drew out a jug, uncorked it, and poured its contents into the kettle.

The old lady did not stir until they brought her a wooden bowlful. When she had tilted the last drop into her mouth, she held it out and smiled.

"You are right, Unzig. The child is good with tea. I'll have another bowl."

After that she took several more, crooning and chuckling to herself, but refusing repeated invitations to lie back and rest. She got out her treasure, a piece of broken mirror, and looked into it, tilting her head and smiling. Then she let her visitors hold it while she drank one more bowl of the tea. Finally she allowed herself to be eased down into the greenery.

Unzig picked up the glass fragment and made swift but careful improvements in her hair and costume. Bexie spread a robe over Owl, then stepped out of the wigwam. She came back carrying a section of long-dead birch, bulky but light. The

wood was so rotted away that hardly any substance was left inside the tough cylinder of bark. She placed it on the boughs and covered it with her skin blanket.

In answer to Unzig's silent question she laid her hands on one shoulder, bent her head on them, and closed her eyes. Then she blinked them open, lifted her head, and pointed her chin at Owl.

Unzig got the message and hurried out herself. Bexie took the mirror, but her primping was soon interrupted by a low squeak from the entrance. Unzig was beckoning. She had found a pine log just the right size and shape but, unlike the birch, solid and heavy. Together they dragged it inside the wigwam and rolled it into position.

Unzig unwrapped her bright blanket, then hesitated, holding it spread in her hands. The pine was soft, moldy, and covered with moss. An ant as red as the blanket came running out of it and looked up at her, waving its feelers distractedly. Suddenly it ran across her moccasin and up her leg, bit her, and ran back into the crumbling wood.

Bexie plucked at her sleeve and nodded toward the door. Unzig put her hand to her mouth and then to the bite, moistening the sore spot. She laid the blanket over the pine and tucked it in. The co-wives skipped silently out into the night.

For a long time there was no motion in the lodge. Dark hours passed. The distant sounds of chanting and drumming grew fainter. Then the door-skin was pushed aside and Sawbill stumbled in. He clung to one of the lodgepoles until his glazed eyes gradually came into focus on the red blanket. Slowly, quietly, he made his way across the floor and crawled in under it.

"I went to sleep in Shypoke's lodge," he whispered. "That is why I am a little late. The young women now-a-days! They have no respect!"

He put an arm around the log.

"You have been a good, obedient wife. You did well not to let Bexie get away. Now I am going to reward you."

He groped at the mossy wood, pulled it toward him, probed its softness. Found an opening, a knothole, perhaps. Wedged blissfully into it.

Within the log the silent warcry shrilled. "To arms, amazons of the ants! The enemy has entered our village! Come, red sisters. It is a good day to die!"

"Ho! Stop that! What have you got in there? Teeth? Needles? Stop it, woman, or I'll leave you! . . . All right, you ungrateful old witch, I'm going to sleep with the second wife."

He rolled over on the boughs, scratching and slapping at the injured part.

"Are you still after me? You'll never win me back that way. You had your chance. Now everything is for Bexie."

He lifted the caribou robe, snuggled in beside the form beneath, and embraced it.

"Ah," he sighed, "the sweet, smooth skin of youth."

He hugged the birch, squeezed hard. It broke in a burst of powdery dust.

Sawbill was suddenly sober. He turned to the third blanketed form.

"Are you another wooden woman?" he shouted. "Have all three of you gone to the dance together?"

He jerked the robe away. The round owl eyes opened. She said something in a rum-rotten murmur. Sawbill needed no further explanation. He dashed down the trail to the dance ground.

One drum was beating. Those people determined to dance their thanks until dawn were still pounding around the worn circle. Others, having slept a little, were returning to take their places. They had all seen Sawbill's wives earlier in the night.

"They were dancing gracefully and with much vigor. You would have been proud. We don't know where they are now."

Sawbill knew.

At Loon's lodge, the red glow of the dying fire revealed a tangle of limbs as naked, motionless, and disorderly as the twisted trunks and branches in a windfall of dead cedar. Loon was snoring, face down, one wing around the first wife, the other thrown out across Bexie's sprawling body. Unzig's tousled head feathers had fallen over her face, but did not hide the smile of the blissful dreamer.

The three lay in a chaos of ashes, blankets, furs, torn clothing, and broken crockery. A mat of woven rushes had been partly ripped from the pole frame of the wigwam and hung, still attached by one corner, close to the wall. Sawbill saw the butt of Loon's old musket protruding from under it. He picked it up, drew out the iron ramrod, and poked it down the barrel, tapping. There was a load in there all right, probably buckshot. Checking further he found that the priming was a little damp. He wiped it out of the pan and replaced it with dry powder

from a flask that had lain near the gun. He swept back the hammer into cocked position and swung the muzzle toward the sleepers.

He stood then, holding the heavy weapon and looking down at them.

A gray hint of sunrise came in through the overhead opening and slid down the slender shaft of smoke, clarifying every detail of the disgraceful scene.

Slowly, thoughtfully, Sawbill lifted the gun barrel and, lowered the hammer with a dull click. He bent and pushed the musket back under the mat but kept the ramrod. He slid one end of it in among glowing embers, then squatted on his heels, waiting. He picked through the jumble on the floor, found a moosehide mitten and put it on his right hand.

He may have been impatient, or his indignation may have subsided a little as the lodge lightened. In any case, the rod was hot when he took it from the coals, but black-hot, not quite red.

Loon's beak was deep in the green bedding, his mouth was open, and he stirred the spruce needles with every breath. His buttocks, cushioned by boughs and bodies, stood up like a hill in a confused wasteland. He was still wearing his belt and his leggings were tied to it, but his breechclout was gone.

With careful, precise, motions, Sawbill knelt beside him, gently lifted his tail feathers, brought the ramrod into position, sighted along it, and pushed it firmly into the puckered opening.

Loon moved, fast. Only slightly more slowly, it seemed to Sawbill, than the load of lead that he might have fired from the musket.

He passed through the wall of the lodge in an explosion of rending bark and wood. Several saplings were broken off as he straightened the curves in the trail. Three dancers were bowled over.

When he hit the river he was travelling so swiftly that, instead of sinking, he ran skittering over the surface leaving a shining track in the dark reflections of the opposite bank. He was flapping his arms hard, and steadily picking up speed. The watchers saw him lift off the water. The ramrod fell with a splash.

His big, flat feet trailed out behind. He circled once above the awakening camp, uttering strange cries. Then he headed south.

"Our revels now are ended," Sawbill told his wives. "Get dressed and get packed."

Ten days later, as the remaining canoes were being loaded at Rat Root, Peboan, Old Man Winter, strolled out of the forest.

"Kind greetings to you all," he said. "And especially to my friend Loon." He looked around. "Where is the dear fellow?"

"He left. In a hurry. We don't think he'll be back until spring."

Peboan had to know the reason for this sudden departure. As the story came out, his genial mood cooled. The trees around the campground froze and cracked like gunshots. Instead of paddling, the people had to cache their canoes and walk over the ice to their winter hunting grounds.

On Sawbill's headland, the family worked hard and steadily, cutting and dragging in firewood. It was well that they did.

Soon enough Peboan came hurrying up the shore. He stood on the cliff, looking down on the lodge and meditating. Then he too went to work.

He chased the deer, the partridge and the big white hares far away. He called in Northwind to blow cold, night and day, so that the holes the women cut in the ice froze before they could put nets into them. He piled snow around the lodge until only a small cone of bark, with blackened poles protruding above it, showed over the drifts.

Then he sat back to watch. But he jumped up often to prowl among the rocks behind the camp trying to think of what other damage he might do. After several weeks he became unable to wait any longer.

"Surely they should all be starved or frozen by this time," he said. "And yet, on this cold night, a little smoke is still coming up. I will pay a friendly call."

He used a snowshoe to shovel down to the door, drew the bearskin aside and stepped in.

"Good evening, cousins," he said, smiling and nodding so that the icicles hanging from his hair tinkled.

"Welcome to this lodge," replied Sawbill. He shivered. "Put another log on, Bexie."

"Don't bother about that on my account," said Peboan. "I'm sweating already."

And indeed they could see water beginning to dribble down his face. Bexie laid the wood on anyway. Peboan continued the conversation.

"Nice weather we're having. Let's hope it lasts."

There was no answer but Northwind's wail as he blew a gust of snow down through the smokehole.

"How've you been, cousin? I hope you're having good hunting. Are you eating well?"

Sawbill was pulling on his parka. When his head poked up out of the hood he answered.

"Oh yes, we all love fish soup. Get some soup for our guest, Bexie. . . . Bexie! . . . Where is that girl?"

"She's never around when she's wanted," said Unzig. "Here, I'll serve the chowder myself."

She got up, keeping the red blanket tightly wrapped around her body. She handed Peboan a bowl and he held it out while she swung the kettle away from the fire and poured. There was a clank as the soup dropped in one frozen mass.

"That's plenty," said Peboan. His jaws crunched the icy chunk. "And just the way I like it. Better go easy on the firewood, though. I wouldn't want you to run out."

Sawbill pulled the hood up around his head and peered out through the long fur. He could see a puddle forming around Peboan.

"You mustn't worry about our wood supply, cousin. I figure we've got enough to last us till the leaves come out. And quite a lot extra. We won't have to cut much next summer."

He thought of the dwindling pile under the snow and wished that his words were true.

Peboan finished the soup and stood up.

"This place is getting too hot."

He went to the entrance and swung back the bearskin so that it caught against the outside bark and timber. Northwind was ready with a snow shoe load of snow. He tossed it swirling in to hiss on the fire and to whiten and chill the people.

At that moment, out from over the lake, they heard a familiar but unexpected cry.

"Scaup, scaup."

Peboan froze.

The harsh sound came again.

"Bluebills. Those nasty little ducks are back already. No wonder it's so hot. Pardon my swift departure, cousins. I hate to eat and run like this, but it's time for me to go north. See you again when the rivers freeze."

He clumped out into the night. Unzig hurried over to the door and pulled the covering back across it, then piled more wood on the fire. The lodge began to warm up again.

Bexie slipped in under the skin and squatted in her place.

"Where have you been, you lazy slut," Unzig inquired politely. "I, the first wife, should not have to do the work when we have company. But that's when you always duck out."

"Scaup," said Bexie. "Scaup, scaup."

Winter continued a long time after that, but the weather had changed. The blizzards were interspersed with mild spells. At last the ice began to shift on the lake. When it broke open the wind piled great slabs of it in a rampart along the shore. One day they heard a genuine scaup. The ducks and geese were returning.

Loon came later. He flew back and forth above the camp, yodelling, but nobody looked up. Finally he flapped off over the treetops. A long strand of laughter hung in the air behind him, echoing against the cliffs and slowly fading over 'Tschgumi.

That spring both of the wives had babies, triplets for Unzig and quadruplets for Bexie. Sawbill noticed that they were covered with dark down, as though every one of them had been rubbed with charcoal. He didn't say anything about that but he did remark that it was a lot of kids for one wigwam.

The mothers took turns, one doing the camp work while the other minded the children. Whoever was in charge would usually lead them down to the water. They were good swimmers. All seven would follow the babysitter in a winding line that rose and fell with the waves. After a lesson from Bexie they arched their bodies, tossed up their toes, and dived way down through the gradually darkening water to level off and skim over the rocky bottom. Soon they were coming up with minnows.

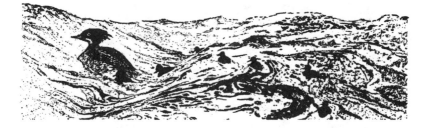

They all enjoyed the fat and fishy summer. The leaves fluttered down from the birches on the cliff, dotting the blue lake and laying a mat of rusty gold around the lodge. One still morning, the swimmers had to break through a rim of ice to get to open water.

"It is time for our annual Rat Root vacation," said Unzig. "We had better leave now so as not to miss any of the religious observances. They do us all good. They and the cultural activities will be so educational for the children. And Sawbill, don't worry about Bexie. I won't let her out of my sight."

The Enemy

Each night, when the evening meal was finished and the fire burned low at the center of the lodge, the grandfather was ready with another story. These were not always about magic, monsters and ghosts. Sometimes he told of conquests as brutal and glorious as the deeds of those other primitive heroes, far on the ringing plains of windy Troy.

"We came west long ago," said Sturgeon Man. "We came from the Eastern Ocean. The Iroquois followed us as wolves follow the deer, killing stragglers, and cutting off small groups. On the shore of 'Tschgumi the ancestors turned and destroyed them.

"When the Sauks and the Foxes attacked the island village our people were too few to fight them on land. We trailed the raiders across the big water, closed in on them when the wind blew, upset their canoes, and broke the heads of those who did not drown."

Sturgeon Man leaned over an imaginary gunwale, swung a phantom warclub, brought it crashing down on the skull of a swimming specter.

"And even now, when the storm spirits move over that part of the lake, you may see them, tossing far out there in the waves, pale canoes paddled by painted ghosts."

The old ones had fought well, too, against trained European soldiers. They had sent a contingent down lakes and rivers and then overland all the way to the bushy ravine in Pennsylvania where the advancing British regulars and their colonial auxiliaries had been met, shattered, and driven into panic flight. The names of Braddock and Washington would have meant nothing

127

to Sturgeon Man, but he knew the story of that long warpath and short fight.

And he could tell how Anishinabe men and women, by guile and by fury, overwhelmed the redcoat soldiers and took the strong fortress that commanded the Straits of the Turtle.

"Those were the people that we came from. You must not forget what they did. Their fires still burn in our wigwams and their smoke hangs over us."

But what particularly fascinated this audience was the familiar account of Sturgeon Man's experience as a warrior. Smoke-Drifting called for it now.

"Tell us again, grandfather, about your own war. Your war with the 'Bwaneg."

"The 'Bwaneg, yes. The white men call them Sioux. They were their enemies as well as ours.

"They were savages, backward in many ways, but fierce and deadly killers. They still are. We had better guns than they did and more shot and powder from our trade with the whites. We kept pushing them west. To the edge of the forest. And then farther. We took this country from them, but it was not easy."

The heaviest fighting had taken place in the hardwood areas, rich in fish, game, rice, and sugar maples, that lay to the south. Dwellers in the cold boreal forest could not ordinarily afford the luxury of war.

"Up here we were too busy keeping ourselves alive to take much time out for killing other people. But even here, the 'Bwaneg returned.

"When I was about your age, He-Rises, I stood beside what they had left of a wigwam just a little down the river from the Wabigoon camp. The bark was still smoldering, and people were dragging out the dead. They had been gutted like deer and scalps, ears, and genitals had been cut off. And the hands of the babies. When I looked at those I was sick.

"I walked back along the trail trying to forget what I had seen. I heard something move in the underbrush. It was a dog. He had an arrow through him, the head on one side, the feathers on the other. He was the only one from the lodge that was still alive.

"Those days were different from these. The men were braver then. And the women were more beautiful."

He stopped quickly, and looked across the fire at Shanod.

"Anishinabe women are always beautiful. But they were beautiful in a different way.

"And the young men. In those times, when an enemy came into our country and harmed our people, the young men were not willing to sit in the wigwams and do nothing."

As Sturgeon Man sat now, in the snow-covered lodge, telling this story to his grandchildren, the vengeance ceremony that he had experienced in his youth—and the events that followed—were still clear in his memory. . . .

It started with drumming, a soft, relentless thunder that called on men to stand together. The deep vibrations were soon repeated in chanting and the beat of dancers' moccasins.

Then a woman came running out into the firelight. She had torn her clothing, sawed off her hair with a knife, and slashed her arms and face.

"You have seen what they did to my son, my daughter-in-law, and my grandchildren."

She threw back her head and gave a long wail. Then she hunched forward and swung around, looking out under her ragged hair from one to another of those in the circle.

"Now, you men! You young men of the Anishinabeg. Which of you is going to kill me a 'Bwan?"

Sturgeon Man, with many others, answered her by smoking the red-feathered war pipe, striking the painted war post, and taking his place in the war dance.

It was known that the old hunter, Crooked Lightning, had fought the Abwaneg when he lived in the flat country beyond the white man's medicine-line. They said that every man was a warrior there.

The young men asked him to be their leader. His southern drawl was so heavy that they could not always understand what he wanted them to do, but he made his preparations well. He sent out messengers carrying the red buckskin hand, the invitation to a war party. Many wanted to come but Crooked Lightning would take no one who was not well armed. This was in the good years when the white men paid well for beaver, and guns were plentiful.

Blue Flag Woman came to him carrying a sawed-off musket.

"With this gun I killed a bear and with it I can kill a 'Bwan. My brother will be one of your war party. I can shoot as well as he or any man. I will come with you."

Crooked Lightning rubbed the sparse hairs on his chin and looked unhappy.

"I have heard of you and of your hunting. I am sure that you would shoot Abwaneg as well as you have shot deer and

129

the bear. But these animals shoot back. They might kill you instead."

"I am not afraid to die."

"I will not take a woman on this long journey."

"I can walk as far as my brother can, and farther. I do not have to tell you, uncle, that there have been great woman warriors among the Anishinabeg."

"I know that well. I fought beside one of them myself. But those with us were experienced fighters, men of firm will and strong self-control. To them she was a comrade, just as though she had been a man. We knew that if any one of us even thought of her womanness, misfortune would befall our war party.

"They are young men who will go with me from this place. They know nothing about war and they think much about women. You might cause jealousy and quarreling among them."

"I will go with you to meet enemies, not lovers. I will give no one of your men cause to be jealous of another."

"You would do worse than that, no matter how good your intentions. The sight of you would pollute their thoughts. They would be thinking about you and the mystery of your body. That must not happen in a war party. It turns the spirit power not only against the offenders, but also against their companions.

"So stay here and provide the meat that will be needed while we are away. I cannot take the risk of having you with us."

She stood looking at him, searching for something else, maybe some kindly weakening in his eyes. Finally she swung the short gun over her shoulder and went away, walking boldly as though she did not care.

When a strong force had come together, Crooked Lightning led the fleet of canoes down many lakes and rivers to the southwest. The women paddled beside them all that first morning, shouting contempt for the Abwaneg and singing kill-them songs. The new warriors were pushing hard to go swiftly over the water and get at those hated ones.

Canoes bearing other men kept coming out from points, bays, and river mouths. They had received the message of the hand and were camped along the route, waiting to join the war party.

They passed through many lakes and streams until these flowed together in one river that brought them at last into a big lake. Not so big as 'Tschgumi, but very big. They couldn't see the other shore.

When they did reach that far shore, it was flat muskeg beyond the sand beach, and here the waterways ended. Everyone was happy to be on ground again, even this trembling earth. They had been paddling for a long time.

They followed the old war road through a broad bog with intervals of forest. The weather was hot, with rain always in the sky. Not much was coming down, but enough to keep this swampy path soft. In the low places it was all a man could do to lift one leg out of the sucking pull of the mud and push it back in again ahead of the other.

Every so often somebody would go down deep and have to be dragged out with a pole or a line. That would have been funny on a soft portage in their country, but not in this place.

So late in the summer the flies and mosquitos had eased at home. Here they buzzed and bit as though spring flowers were blooming.

On the third night that they camped on this trail, one of the young men stood up beside the fire and spoke to the others.

"I never thought that the world was so big nor that the 'Bwaneg lived on the other side of it. The rice will soon be ripening. If we keep on walking west much longer we will be late for the harvest and our families may starve next winter. Also, my moccasins are wearing thin and I am tired of this kind of war.

"I will go home to the lakes tomorrow. I advise the rest of you to come with me."

In the morning many people turned back. But more went on with Crooked Lightning. They were still a strong war party.

They came up into a higher country, with tall grass, scattered swamps and lakes, and wandering belts of timber. This was a no-man's-land where the hunters of neither tribe were safe. Nobody hunted it much. The animals had fattened and multiplied. They camped, made meat, ate what they wanted, and cached the rest for the return trip. Then they walked on to the west.

One evening Sturgeon Man, with some of the others, crouched in scanty brush and peered out at a small circle of skin-covered tipis on the edge of the prairie. Looking back he could see the tree line. It stretched out to the south and the north like the shore of a great lake.

Crooked Lightning, keeping low and silent in the long grass, came in beside him. He was speaking in signs and whispers.

"The scouts who found this encampment have said that its hunters are away. This is good.

"At the first light of dawn, I will give the signal shout. Several men will be waiting to scatter the horse herd. The rest of us will rush the village. The boys there, and the old men, will fight. The Abwaneg will always fight. But this time probably without guns, or without many guns. The hunters will have them, and most of the ammunition.

"Shoot carefully and then go in fast. We should be able to overrun all who will try to stop us without losing anybody of ours. Then we must wipe out every person in the camp. The men first, then immediately the women, and then the children. By that time it will be light enough to find any that escape into the grass.

"Sleep now and be ready at daylight."

He started to leave, then turned back.

"Do not delay about the women. They are unsafe."

He slipped away to the next group, going as quietly as he had come. There was no sound after that from any of the Anishinabeg, but Sturgeon Man could hear the Abwaneg moving about and talking.

The women were bending over the cooking fires and the children were playing or scuffling a little, waiting for the food. After they had eaten, most of the people went into the tipis, but three old men sat for a long time by a fire. When it was quite dark Sturgeon Man crept in close.

One of the elders had a big nose and a long, flat face. He must have been saying funny things. He kept moving his hands and sometimes pointing. Then the other two would take the pipes out of their mouths and laugh. Sturgeon Man could understand nothing of their strange, throaty language, but they did not look very different from old men by the fire at home.

He came back to the others and waited there through the night, too excited to sleep.

When the stars began to fade he heard the war-shout. There was a thunder of hoofs as the horses stampeded. People were running out of the tipis, most of them naked from the sleeping robes, not dressed a little as sleepers would have been in the north.

All around him the Anishinabeg were shooting. Sturgeon Man fired with the others. He knew that he should pick out one man, but he just aimed at the mass. Then he threw down the empty musket, drew his knife, and ran forward.

A tipi had been knocked over in the rush, a pile of hides and poles. He was running as hard as he could and it was right in his way. As he bent to jump over it a man with shaggy white hair rose out of it, swinging a stone-headed war club. He was the one with the big nose and the flat face, but he was not joking now. That evil old man was trying to kill him.

He tried to stop, skidded into the wreckage, and fell. He rolled over, his hand slipping on the leather lodge covering, not able to get up quickly enough. He saw the stone swing down at his head.

There was an explosion from behind him. The Abwan fell across him, knocking him flat on the ground again. Sturgeon Man struggled against him but the old man was not trying to kill anybody now. He was jerking a little and bright red blood was coming out of his chest. Another Anishinabe had held his fire.

He got to his feet and stood there, glad to be still alive, uncertain what to do next. An arrow sang low above him.

The Abwaneg, boys and elders, fighting with bows, spears, and axes, were holding back the Anishinabeg like a mass of broken ice that heaves and cracks and groans as it stops the swelling river for a little while before it is swept away.

Beyond them he could see women running. They were carrying babies and herding the other children ahead of them, pushing and dragging the smaller ones for speed.

He knew that something had gone wrong. The enemy were not many and they had no guns. But they had not been wiped out in the first rush as Crooked Lightning had ordered. Others, like him, must have fired without really aiming.

He couldn't find his knife, but he picked up the war club. Some of the young men had dropped back to reload their muskets. He joined them as they hurried into the fight again.

He saw an old Abwan turn and look behind him. Now there were no more women or children in sight. He called something to the others. The ice jam broke. An Anishinabe flood roared through the empty village.

Those of the enemy still on their feet were running. Some of them were holding up others who stumbled, or carrying bodies whose feet dragged in the dust. Those who went last were moving quickly, but turned a little to keep watch, with weapons still ready. They disappeared into the long grass and low hills.

Crooked Lightning was running after them, calling for everybody else to follow. Sturgeon Man and several others started to, but not very swiftly. The rest just stood and watched.

The old man came back, very angry.

"Have we come so far, then, to kill so few? Will you let yourselves be beaten by kids and grandfathers?"

They stood there, breathing hard from the fighting. No one answered and no one moved.

Crooked Lightning swung his arm in a violent gesture of contempt.

"I used to hear it said that the men of the spruce forests were not warriors but bush rabbits. I didn't believe it then. Now I know that it is true. A southern Anishinabe war party would not stop while a single Abwan stayed alive."

It was a while before someone answered.

"The 'Bwaneg are devils. We caught them naked, asleep, and almost unarmed. But even the women knew just what to do. Those old men must have fought in many battles. If we follow them they will probably lay a trap for us. They might kill us all."

Another spoke quickly. "Gagonce is dead, Gwekabi's arm is broken, and several have been wounded. But I don't think that we have been beaten. See, we have taken scalps."

They had the hair of four males, of one woman who had been cut off from the flight, and the scalp of her new baby.

That one was like gosling down. And the horse-chasers had brought in a captive, a girl a little younger than Sturgeon Man, who had been tending the herd.

"We have enough for a good victory dance. And enough to show the 'Bwaneg that they can't just come up and kill our people in the north and go back without getting hurt themselves. We hit more of them than we have scalps. They carried away dead and wounded."

"It would do no good to walk farther into that strange country, all grass. See how the wind blows waves over it as though it were water. There is no way to know what kind of evil spirits may be waiting for us in such deadly emptiness."

Crooked Lightning was still very angry. Seeing the captive did not make him feel any better.

"I told you to kill all of those. You well know that they bring misfortune to a war party. Cut her throat now!"

"The fighting is finished, uncle. We have had our misfortune and our good fortune. We are going home and we will take her with us."

The old man gave a sour little snort.

"The fighting may not be finished yet. We are a long way from the canoes. And do not think that this one is like an Anishinabe woman. These are vicious. All of them. Whenever we have allowed one to live she has made bad trouble."

A man had been leading the captive with a rawhide line around her neck.

"She is not big enough or old enough to be dangerous. She will do whatever I want her to do. See, she has already learned to obey the cord."

He twitched it and she stepped quickly ahead.

"I will watch her myself to make sure that she does nobody any harm."

Crooked Lightning spat on the ground and turned away.

Another of the men called after him. "There is no need to worry, uncle. We will kill her if she gives us any trouble along the way. If she gets to the rice camp the women will finish her off at the ceremony."

Crooked Lightning did not look back.

A healer bound up the wounds. The dead one was wrapped in a blanket and slung from a carrying-pole. Some took what they wanted of the scattered village possessions, but there wasn't much that they could use.

Sturgeon Man went back and found his knife and musket. He was thinking about those hunters, wondering when they might be getting home. Maybe others had the same thought. Anyway, they soon started back to the east, and they walked fast.

Again the long march, the heat, the aching feet, the biting flies. It was as though the fight had been a dream. Except that the blanketed bundle that had been Gagonce swung and jolted as it was carried on the pole. And there was the captive, hauled along by the thong around her neck and beaten with sticks whenever she failed to keep the swift pace.

That night they stopped in thickening forest growth. Crooked Lightning had posted scouts along the back trail and around the camp. He had the corpse washed and a grave dug in the path. Gagonce's weapons and sacred pipe were placed beside him so that their souls would go with his. A fire was built over the newly turned earth and a hasty burial feast was eaten.

The girl had been crouching, silent, in the shadows. She was an enemy, and any of the Anishinabeg might scalp or stab her at will. Now she was dragged out into the firelight. Someone tore at her gown.

Crooked Lightning became angry again. Even more angry than he had been after the battle.

"So, it comes to this. You know well how dangerous it is to sully the purity of a war party's purpose by even thinking about woman. And especially about her mysterious wound that gives life to the world and bleeds with the changing moon. The Bear-Mother guards that sacred cave. A man must not go into it before a bear hunt or a battle. To do so may bring misfortune to the enterprise and death or injury to those who take part in it.

"Do not think that such punishment must be something far away. It may already be hiding behind those bushes that shine against the edge of the darkness.

"If you have forgotten the Abwaneg, be sure that the Abwaneg have not forgotten you. At this time you should be lying in ambush along the back trail, not lying with a woman."

But the young men were not listening to his stream of scold. They had stretched the girl on the ground. Three of them held her while the others, one after another, lowered themselves upon her. Those who had finished went out to relieve the scouts so that they might have their turns. Even Gwekabi, carefully maneuvering the splinted arm, took his painful pleasure.

Sturgeon Man stood back at first, shaken by Crooked Light-ning's words. But he forgot them as he watched the men and the girl. He had become eager, excited and a little frightened, but not of the Abwaneg. He had never entered a woman.

When his turn came he pushed aside his breech clout and came down on the raw, shuddering body. She had ceased strug-gling. No one had to hold her now.

His long hair fell around her face, shutting them off from the others. Her eyes, big with pain and fear, looked up at him. She winced as he clumsily prodded, not finding the opening at first. When he did find it, he emptied himself quickly and moved aside to make room for the next man.

During the following days she was treated less roughly. No one wanted to kill her. She was so stiff and sore that she was clearly unable to keep up with the men, no matter how they might jerk on her neck cord or switch her legs. So they made a blanket litter and carried her. But they took their turns with her again each night. Sturgeon Man was still eager and excited, but no longer frightened.

They came back through the parkland, the thickening forest, and into the swamp country. The cached meat was only a little rotten and they ate it rather than take time to hunt. One evening the word went out that they would reach the canoes next day.

Crooked Lightning had trouble getting sentries to go out to the posts that night. The young men said that the Abwan camp had been a small one, and that even if the hunters had come in, they would be too few to attack so strong a party. The Anishinabeg had put all these days of fast travel between them and the enemy. They did not think that they need worry now about a counterattack. And they were very tired.

Sturgeon Man agreed to take a watch later in the night if he could sleep first. Soon enough the other man woke him, pointed out the way he was to go, and lay down in the vacant spot by the embers of the fire.

The moon was a slim bent bow in the sky, but there was enough light to get through that flat and thinly timbered coun-try. Out here alone, the position didn't seem quite so secure as it had in the camp. It came to Sturgeon Man now that if the enemy were following, tonight would be their last opportunity to attack.

He looked around for a rock outcropping that would con-ceal him and, if necessary, stop a bullet. The friendly stone that had always been so plentiful in the forest was not to be found here. He finally settled for a clump of distorted and interwoven alder trunks. The ground beneath them was dry at this season. They gave a little concealment and provided a good view of some open grassland. It was too dark to see much out there now, but he would command this natural clearing at the first daylight.

He had always loaded his musket with the usual hunting measure. Now he doubled the amount of powder, took up a handful of heavy shot and paused, hefting the rough lead spheres and considering. He had never fired such a combination. Would it break the breech? Not if he didn't have to shoot. And if the Abwaneg did come, he wanted something that would do plenty of damage. He dropped the shot into the barrel, tamped the charge solidly home, primed the pan, and sat down in his cover.

Time passed slowly at first. Several times he thought that someone was out there in the grass, and twice he raised the musket. Each of these alarms ended when he located some night animal or realized that it was only a tree shadow that had seemed to move.

After an hour of this sitting he began to feel the chill of the late summer night. He was glad that he had had the foresight to bring a thick moose-hide hunting shirt. He put it on, tying it tight with the front flaps overlapping. He felt more comfortable then and less troubled by either the cold or any possible enemies that the shadows might conceal. He may even have dozed a little.

A musket roared. Close to him, the next post in the line of scouts. He heard some one, more than one, run past him toward the camp. He strained to see. He could make out nothing in the open glade before him.

He wondered whether he should shoot into the darkness for a warning. No, they would not be sleeping now.

He heard a scatter of shots from the camp, some shouting, a few more shots, and then silence. He dropped low in the sheltering brush and stared between the kinky alders in that direction.

Some gray light was opening the sky now, and he saw the Abwan as soon as he came out of the trees. He was running lightly, alert, gun muzzle swinging as he looked to the right and the left. Sturgeon Man lay silent, not moving, hardly breathing.

138

Still the runner must have caught some warning, some message of his presence. Suddenly he stopped, face and gun pointing toward the Anishinabe. He stood there, shifting his head a little, trying to make out what might be concealed in the alder thicket. Then he walked cautiously toward it.

Sturgeon Man dared not raise his musket. Any movement would give him away. The enemy, alert, ready, clearly an experienced warrior, was closing in carefully, with his finger on the trigger.

There was the sound of breaking branches behind him. A smaller person came struggling through the brush, hobbling, trying painfully to run. It was the captive. She limped across the clearing toward them, then tripped and fell.

Even a seasoned warrior can make a mistake. This one looked away, turned from the thicket, took a step back to give help or encouragement.

Sturgeon Man did not fire blindly as he had in his first fight. He rose to a kneeling position, took careful aim, and gently drew back the trigger.

The recoil from the heavy load flung him backwards. Awkwardly, painfully, he sat up and then got to his feet. He could see, through the cloud of smoke, that he had hit his mark. The fierce raider had become a bundle of torn rags and bloody meat.

The girl struggled up, looked down at the fallen man, and gave a moaning cry. She stood there a moment, her head drooping, then swung wildly about and continued her flight.

Sturgeon Man's ears were ringing, and his shoulder ached from the jolt of the blast, but he dashed from his hiding place to cut off her escape. He was still holding the empty musket.

She tried to dodge but he siezed the front of her dress with his free hand, checking her momentum and twisting the garment to force her down.

She flung herself backward, jerking desperately, but could not break his grip. He saw something gleam in her hand. She slashed up at him like a steel-gripped lynx when the careless trapper, raising his club, leans too far forward. He felt a sharp, cold point rip his flesh and grate along a rib.

The pain and the amazing impact of the blow staggered him. Through the shock of it he felt a violent jerking. His head was being shaken backward and forward as she wrenched and pushed at a stub that projected from his reeling body.

He swung the gun barrel as hard as he could at that short distance. It caught her beside the head and she dropped. He

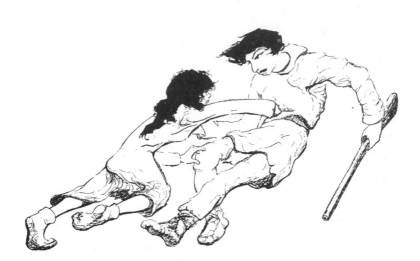

staggered back, felt blood running down his side, but stayed on his feet.

Beside her lay part of an arrow shaft with the iron head attached. Somehow she had stolen and hidden it and honed it to a vicious edge. But the double thickness of stout moosehide had turned and slowed the point, then caught one of the barbs as she tried to withdraw it for another thrust.

She was sitting up, holding her head, when men came following her tracks from the camp. Sturgeon Man, weakened and badly shaken, but beginning to feel very proud, stood over her, ready to hit her again if she showed any more fight.

When the others had taken her by the arms and dragged her away he walked over the to the man he had shot. The Abwan's body had been torn open by the heavy load of slugs at close range. Sturgeon Man drew his knife and grasped the hair. Hacking, sawing and jerking, he got off most of the scalp. It could not be called a skilled job, or tidy. But, as he stood with the matted thing dripping in his hand, it filled him with the ecstacy of sudden, unexpected, but unchallengeable achievement.

At the camp, the healer examined his wound, sucked it, spat out blood, performed a short ceremony over it, applied a herbal poultice and bandaged it. He told Sturgeon Man that he would be able to walk without assistance but must not try to carry a pack on the trail nor paddle or portage a canoe when they got to the water.

Crooked Lightning said that the attack had been made by only a few men, probably a small party of hunters that had come back to the village before the others. They might have been following close for several days and attacked that night because it had become clear that the main body would not arrive in time to cut off the forest men from the water.

They had overrun and knifed down the sentry, but not before he got off the warning shot. Another of the Anishinabeg had been shot through the thigh, a serious wound but not likely to be fatal. Several of the young men believed that they had made hits, and that the Abwaneg had carried away some dead or wounded, but they could not be certain. Anyway, one enemy was dead for sure, and the rescue attempt had failed. It could have been much worse.

Crooked Lightning looked at Sturgeon Man, smiling a little.

"This one has done well. He is not one of the bush rabbits. And now he understands Abwan women."

The march started quickly that morning. Crooked Lightning had to speak scornfully, shaming them into taking time to bury the sentry. The retreat went on through the heat of the day, covered now by willing scouts. They were all happy when, in the late afternoon, they reached the shore without being attacked again. The canoes were hurriedly carried across the beach and loaded. Only when the paddles dipped and the rhythm of the lake moved under them did they feel safe. The land-lubberly Abwaneg could not get at them here.

The girl's head was badly swollen but she rested in the canoe, laying back against a pack. There was less need to hurry now, and she was able to get over the portages on her own feet.

The return voyage ended at the rice camp in the moon of the shining leaf. The people had been called to the shore by watchers. They stared against the glare of the setting sun, counting the paddlers in the approaching canoes, wondering who the missing ones would be.

There was wailing for the two dead warriors but also dancing, and songs of triumph. The scalps came up from the canoes first, bouncing and fluttering on poles. Behind them stumbled the captive, jerked again by the noose around her neck.

The woman whose son and grandchildren had been massacred came running into the camp circle, waving a chunk of birch firewood. She swung it at the Abwan. The girl shrank back, putting up her arm. The first blow knocked down that defense and the second struck her head, driving her to the ground. For a few moments the woman stood over her, breathing heavily, her eyes gleaming out through the hair that had fallen across her face. Then she bent down and began to batter the unresisting figure beneath her.

She would have pounded the life out if Sturgeon Man and others of the war party had not intervened. They took the club away and held the avenger back from the flattened body.

That was not a polite thing to do. Who had a better right to kill the captive than the bereaved mother-grandmother? There were murmurs of disapproval from the crowd.

The young men felt shame. They knew that they were behaving badly, but they held the woman anyway, as gently as they could, until she gave up the struggle and sank down weeping.

Others showed their hatred of the Abwaneg by kicking her and jabbing her with pointed sticks. She lay sprawled, her face pushed into the earth, and did not move.

A little boy came running up with a glowing coal in a short cleft stick and held it to her back where her dress had been torn away. That seemed to bring her to life. She raised herself a little. Her face was so caked with blood and dirt that she did not look like a person, but like some animal that has been blasted with buckshot. Out of that dark smear, the whites of her eyes gleamed wildly. Then her arms gave way and she dropped back to the ground.

This was the time when attention was shifting from the enemy to the Anishinabeg fighters. The people were gathering around them, an excited audience, anxious to hear their accounts.

Sturgeon Man went to stand with the others, then stepped back to where the girl was lying. The boy was drawing a pale design on her skin, only stopping when he had to blow on the coal to keep it glowing. Fascinated with this artistic effort and soothed by the smell of scorched flesh, he had not noticed the crowd moving away.

Sturgeon Man took the stick gently from his hand and tossed it, in a shining curve, through the darkness and into the fire.

"Come, little brother. We will tell you about the war."

The story of the battle and the repulsed counterattack was acted out with brandished weapons and ferocious looks as each man described his own actions. They spoke, to the beat of the truth-demanding drum, with pride and passion, but honestly, careful not to make any false claim.

Sturgeon Man told and showed how he had killed the raider and recaptured the prisoner. The women responded with cries of pleasure, and some of them circled around him with prancing little steps. It was a magnificent moment.

The triumph ceremony went on for a long time. The drumming, dancing and singing continued. Even the smallest children insisted on handling the scalps and striking the fallen enemy. At last they all had stopped, exhausted, standing around her.

Someone bored into her back, twisting a sharpened stick. She did not move.

"I think that she is dead now."

"Let us lay her on the fire and find out."

"I will show you how to tell," said one of the older men. He bent over the girl, took an arm, slashed it with a knife, and dropped it.

"Be quiet and listen."

The people were standing around her blocking the light from the fire so that Sturgeon Man could no longer see her. But he could hear the rhythmic spurts of blood striking the dry leaves. Zit . . . zit . . . zit.

The man wiped his blade.

"She is alive still. But that will take care of her. There is no need to bother with her further."

"Get her legs," Sturgeon Man said to one of his friends. "You and I will carry her to the medicine woman."

"Let her lie," the knife man snarled. "They killed our people."

Sturgeon Man grasped her under the arms and tried to lift, but sharp pain struck the partly-healed wound. He let the shoulders down, and the crowd moved in. He faced them, pretending to stand strong.

Another member of the war party took his place at the girl's head and they carried her away from the fire. An indignant group followed, speaking loudly of those who loved the Abwaneg.

Keewidnok, Woman-of-the-North-Wind, put aside her sleeping robes and got up as they carried the body into her lodge. She had watched the triumph ceremony for a while and had then gone home to bed. She was not pleased with what they had brought her.

"I didn't hit her and I don't want to have anything to do with her now. Take her somewhere else. . . . But wait."

She had seen the fresh stain on Sturgeon Man's shirt.

"I don't think that's her blood."

She stepped closer and pulled the garment up.

"You need attention, young man. Take the Abwan away, you others, and I will dress this wound."

She lifted the door covering and motioned them out. The crowd made a sound like a she-bear when the hunter prods her with a pointed pole to get her out of the winter den.

"Give her to us," a woman called. "We will do with her as her people did to our people."

The bearers stopped in the doorway, looking their question at the medicine woman. Sturgeon Man lifted the girl's left arm to show the bright rhythm of the flowing blood.

"She needs your healing more than I do. And she needs to stay a little while in your lodge. Take care of her first. Then, perhaps, these people will have gone away and she can be brought somewhere else and you can see to my small hurt."

North-Wind hesitated. There was more growling from outside. She spread a robe on bough bedding. "Lay her here, then.

"My husband and my daugher are away, so I will need help. You two who are whole, stand outside the door and let no one come in. You, Cut-side, since your hurt is little and not in a hurry to be mended, stay with me and I will tell you what to do."

She cut away the few shreds that remained of the young woman's sleeve, then took Sturgeon Man's hand and guided it to a point on the upper arm.

"Press here. . . . Harder, and not just with a finger. Use the heel of your hand."

He pushed down hard and the red fountain subsided.

The medicine woman was chanting now, but not taking time for a real healing ceremony. That surprised him, but he said nothing. She filled a kettle with water, poured something into it from a bark kettle, and hung it over the fire. She pushed a roll of tightly twisted birch bark into a split stick, dipped the bark into the flame, and put the stick into Sturgeon Man's free hand.

"Keep pressing, but hold that to light what I will do."

She knelt beside the girl and squeezed her mouth open. Her fingers searched inside and brought out some pebbles and a tooth in a smear of mud and bloody froth.

A moccasin still clung to one foot. She removed that and what clothing the crowd had left. Quickly she went over the torn and battered body. She packed another badly bleeding gash with some material that looked like dried moss, and bound a piece of soft doeskin over it. Next she turned back to the wound in the arm.

"Good. But keep pressing until I tell you to stop."

She opened another bark container, this one very small and tightly sealed. From it she tapped a brown powder into the palm of her hand. She turned the woman's head to one side and held the powder under her nostrils. Sturgeon Man could smell the bitter strength rising out of it.

He saw the captive's eyelids open. She looked at the flaring torch, at North-Wind's sharp knife, at the faces hanging over her, and at the long, sinister shadows that moved above them across the poles and bark of the wigwam wall. Her eyes took on a defiant intensity and her lips pressed tight together. Sturgeon Man could see that she was preparing herself for the final cutting.

The medicine woman turned to the arm again.

"The bleeding has stopped. Bring me the kettle. That torch will not burn much longer. Light another. And hold a piece of bark to keep it from shining in my eyes."

She added a little cold water to the kettle, tested it with a finger, washed the wound in the arm and bandaged it. Then she leaned over the girl and put a hand on her shoulder, speaking softly.

"You cannot understand my words but I hope you know that we are trying to keep you alive."

She spoke next with some of the sign language but mostly with her own gestures and facial expressions. Sturgeon Man was able to follow her meaning fairly well, and he could see that the Abwan understood her too. North-Wind was asking her to let her know at which points the pain was sharpest.

Starting with the scalp she moved down, checking every part, not hurrying this time. She found the head swollen, bleeding, and lacerated but the skull not broken. She washed and stitched the torn scalp.

She watched the expansion and contraction of the chest for a few moments, then pressed in lightly from the sides. The girl flinched with sudden pain. North-Wind bathed her body then, and bound the cracked ribs.

She went over her belly, pressing lightly, questioning, getting murmured answers now. She squeezed, down on the tops of the hip bones, very gently at first, then harder. Sturgeon Man could see that she was pleased to get no sound or shudder.

"Now take her hip and shoulder and turn her over. Roll her like a log, but slowly, carefully."

As Sturgeon Man turned the body, North-Wind held the head, steadying it to keep it from swinging to either side. She washed the girl's back. Then her hands moved over it, palpating, searching, gently insistent. She put cold, wet, medicated compresses on the burns. She signed for fingers and toes to be wiggled against her appraising palm. She checked the bones of arms, legs, hands and feet.

Her fingers running over the right forearm stopped, went back, pressed a little. The patient said something unintelligible but agonized. North-Wind investigated further.

"The bone is cracked. . . . The grandmother must have put all the strength she had into that first blow."

She told Sturgeon Man to heat a sheet of birch bark. While he held it close to the fire she set the break, smeared the arm with bear grease and wrapped it in a piece of blanket. She bent the hot bark around it and had the young man hold it tight while she bound it in place. As it cooled, it formed a fitted, rigid splint. Two broken fingers were splinted with thin strips of cedar.

North-Wind dressed the other wounds, stitched up the worst and bandaged them. She salved the bruises and put more cold water on the burns.

Then she spread a blanket over that patient and turned to Sturgeon Man. She treated and bandaged his injury, and handed him a little wooden figure.

"This is a sacred thing, a talisman. Touch it to your wound when you first wake, each morning for twenty mornings. During that time do not lift anything heavy. Especially, do not lift any more women. That is a necessary part of the charm. On the twenty-first day bring the talisman back to me so that it can heal others."

They heard one of the young men at the entrance speak firmly, telling someone to stand back.

"You had better leave this one here for the rest of the night. In the morning, though, you must take her away. Now go home and sleep, and the two at the door also. But first, get some other of your child-warriors to keep the noisy people away from my lodge. I will not be bothered out of my bedding again tonight."

He waked others and found several who would leave their robes and come. The crowd was quieter now, and some were going away. The two young men left who had stood guard first. Sturgeon Man walked slowly back past the embers of dying fires to his parents' lodge.

When he came back in the morning the doctor met him at the door opening.

"The girl had a good night. I think that she will be all right, but she's not yet well enough to be moved. I will keep her for a few days. The people calmed down after a while and went home to bed, so I sent the guards away.

"How about you, are you having any more trouble with your little hurt? . . . Good. Blackduck got back early this morning so I won't need any more protection."

Sturgeon Man did not want to seem too much interested in the welfare of an Abwan, nor to bother the medicine woman more than was necessary, but after several days he began to walk past her lodge from time to time, or within sight of it.

On one of these investigative strolls he saw someone, warmly wrapped and with a bandaged head, reclining against a back-rest where the sun came through an opening in the pines before the wigwam. Not far away, Blackduck was using a crooked knife to shape an axe handle from a stick of birch. He got up quickly, putting down the knife but not the stick, and stepped in front of the invalid.

"This woman is no longer an enemy."

"I know that, uncle. I have not come to do her harm."

"Good. Some of the people have been slow to understand." He sat down and went back to work, but kept a watchful eye on the younger man.

Sturgeon Man turned toward the girl, closed his hands and crossed his wrists over his chest in what he had heard was the western sign-word for kind feelings and respect. She looked up at him and raised a splinted hand in acknowledgment. Her eyes were good and the corner of her mouth turn up in a little smile where it was not covered by the wrappings.

This was all the communication they could manage that morning, but he stood beside her for a while until North-Wind saw him and called him into the lodge to inspect his wound.

"It is healing well. So is the captive. She is still weak but she will recover. I have decided to keep her as a servant. She seems to be smart enough and I don't think that she will be dangerous. She may be useful to me."

As time passed, Sturgeon Man noted that North-Wind was not disappointed. The captive did indeed turn out to be useful. As soon as she was well enough she took over the woman's work around the lodge. She picked up the language quickly, although she never lost her heavy Abwan accent. Her mistress began to assign her nursing duties and care of the sick.

They left the rice camps for the hunting grounds, and Sturgeon Man did not see North-Wind or her servant again that winter. When the people came together at the sugar bush in the spring he learned that she had been taken into the family as a daughter. She had been given the name of Wabanaquayash, Dawn Sailing, in recognition of her beginning life as an Anishinabe.

North-Wind's other daughter had never shown much interest in healing, so Dawn Sailing became increasingly important to her new mother.

She grew familiar with the *materia medica* of the woods Indians. She learned to gather and process the plant, mineral, and animal ingredients for each of these in its proper season.

Under North-Wind's guidance, she made healing poultices from aspen bark and flute reed. She cut up pine bark and the inner bark of the wild cherry, then boiled and mashed them for wounds. Hemlock bark and cinquefoil on duck down stopped bleeding. She brewed water lily roots into a tea to cure diarrhea, to be gargled for sore throat, and to be applied as a salve for boils. She dried and crumbled the leaves of fireweed to heal burns. She combined wild ginger and spikenard to make a poultice for broken bones. She prepared deer tendons and basswood fibers for North-Wind to use as sutures in her surgery. Bear's grease was the base for many cures and medicinal lotions, especially valued because the bear too is a healer, and can mend wounds or sores by licking or by the application of those mysterious remedies that only he understands.

In time, Dawn Sailing was able to prescribe an emetic, or a medicated steam bath, let blood, pull an abscessed tooth, give an enema with a deer bladder and a hollow reed, set a broken bone or ease a difficult birth. She could open a frozen toe and rub into it the inner bark of tamarack to prevent mortification. Or, if it was too far gone to save, she would cut it off and cauterize the stump with a hot iron. Several times she helped North-Wind amputate a hand, a foot, or a limb.

The old doctor did not consider herself much of a conjuror. Nursing, surgery, and healing with natural balms were done by people of either sex. Treatment of the sick with charms and ceremonies was, in most cases, carried out by a male shaman. But any physician sometimes needs supernatural help.

North-Wind taught Dawn Sailing how to consult with her drum, beating it, questioning it, and listening carefully to its answer.

"Always speak respectfully to the drum. If it won't talk, don't try to force it. It usually wants to be kind to people and to help in diagnoses, but pushing an unwilling drum can bring much harm."

When Dawn Sailing became skilled and understanding in this work, she was allowed to use her mother's ancient drum stick, carved with a loon's head by some craftsman-magician of forgotten times. Later, North-Wind taught her a few simple incantations that she had found effective for certain maladies. With their herbal medicines and this minor magic they probably cured a somewhat better percentage of their patients than did the white doctors of that time.

Young men came bringing gifts. Among them was Sturgeon Man. Dawn Sailing looked on him with favor. He waited outside

149

the door at night until she came out. She stood with him under his blanket and they talked in low voices until she was summoned back into the lodge by alert parental authority. If all had been well in that lodge she would probably have married him.

But North-Wind was ailing now with some strange malady. She had grown thin in a time of plenty. A sour pain burned steadily in her stomach. Lines ran out from her mouth and left deep creases in the transparent skin of her face. Neither she nor Dawn Sailing could find a remedy. The younger woman felt that she should not, at this time, leave her for marriage.

Gradually she was taking over the practice. This was not so profitable as it may sound. A medicine woman was respected, but was not paid much for her services. Usually she would be given food or some small present.

The old doctor grew weaker. Often now she was wrenched by sudden, intense agony. Clearly, someone was practicing sorcery against her.

All her life she had helped others. Blackduck discussed the question with the two daughters, but they could think of no person who would wish her this misery.

They sent for a wabeno, a calm, thoughtful man with an outstanding reputation for difficult cures. For a day and a night he danced, drummed, and chanted. He tried to suck out the evil spirit through a bone tube. Then, in a low voice, he told the family that it was not in his power to draw the thing from North-Wind's body and that there was nothing more to be done except to make her as comfortable as possible.

Dawn Sailing cared for her, watched over her, and gave her medicines to ease the pain a little, while they waited for Pauguk, old death. North-Wind looked like him by this time and was ready to welcome him. But he seemed to feel that, now that he was sure of her, there was no need to hurry.

Months passed, a year. She lay flat and silent, never stirring except when Dawn Sailing lifted her to give her drink and what little food she would take, or to clean her.

By the time death did arrive, the older daughter was married, and so was Sturgeon Man. Dawn Sailing went on living in Blackduck's lodge, cooking the meat and dressing the hides of the deer and moose he brought in, and treating the sick and injured.

She was almost twenty now, rather old for a single woman in this primitive society. Eventually, though, she found the right man. Her husband was a skilled hunter who already had two capable and industrious wives.

Some Anishinabe women were beginning to take on the Saganash prejudice against polygamy, but Dawn Sailing could see its advantages. Now she would be able to devote most of her time to her patients and to a study of the darker mysteries, especially the defences against such witchcraft as had killed her foster mother.

Several years later, at the end of the sugar season, she took her infant son on the long journey to the hunting grounds of her western relatives. She hoped to find her other parents still alive, or at least to visit her sister.

There was much gossip about this during the berry picking. The women were inclined to agree that her husband had been a fool to let her go. When the rice was ripe for harvest and she had still not returned they were sure that they had seen the last of Dawn Sailing. But just before the waterways froze, she came paddling back with many gifts and a big pack of healing herbs from the prairie. The baby was propped against the thwart before her in a strangely carved Abwan tikinagon.

They had come home.